MW00989102

"*Benchmarking in the Public and Nonprofit Sectors* is a welcome addition to the literature and practice of performance management in public and nonprofit organizations. The authors combine the principles of benchmarking with their real-life experience improving performance in agencies around the world. This is an important management tool for government and nonprofit managers to make their agencies more effective, efficient, and responsive to their constituencies."
　　　　　　　　　　　—W. David Patton, director, Center for Public Policy and
　　　　　　　　　　　Administration, University of Utah

"The benchmarking methods offered by Keehley and Abercrombie resulted in tangible results for our program participants. We have integrated benchmarking into many of our executive development programs so future leaders can improve performance through the use of twenty-first century tools."
　　　　　　　　　　　—Jerry Ice, chief executive officer, Graduate School, USDA

"Keehley and Abercrombie offer extensive tools and examples for successful benchmarking—focused techniques that can inspire both new and experienced managers to use benchmarking. The book's emphasis on accountable and transparent benchmarking processes is relevant from local to global levels and spans from Scotland to Guam. Managers, analysts, and auditors will each find value in this important book."
　　　　　　　　　　　—Drummond Kahn, director of audit services, City of Portland, Oregon

"The first edition of *Benchmarking in the Public and Nonprofit* Sectors was an important book because it was the first to seriously address benchmarking in ways that were useful to students of and practitioners in the public sector. The second edition not only updates this valuable volume, but also expands its coverage into the distinctive world of nonprofit organizations. Keehley and Abercrombie have done a wonderful job of keeping the book focused on its primary purpose. *Benchmarking* is for thoughtful practitioners who want to initiate or improve organizational performance. It is practical and useful. *Benchmarking* is solidly grounded in theory, but the authors don't let theory get in the way with practice. If there is one book on benchmarking that belongs on the desks of public agency and nonprofit organization managers, it is this one."
　　　　　　　　　　　—J. Steven Ott, dean, College of Social and Behavioral Science, and
　　　　　　　　　　　professor, Department of Political Science, University of Utah

Instructors are invited to view and download
the supplementary Instructor's Guide for
Benchmarking in the Public and Nonprofit Sectors,
Second Edition.

The Instructor's Guide is available FREE online.
If you would like to download and print out an
electronic copy of the Instructor's Guide, please visit
www.wiley.com/college/keehley

Benchmarking in the Public and Nonprofit Sectors

BEST PRACTICES FOR ACHIEVING PERFORMANCE BREAKTHROUGHS

Second Edition

Patricia Keehley, Ph.D.
Neil N. Abercrombie

JOSSEY-BASS
A Wiley Imprint
www.josseybass.com

Published by Jossey-Bass
A Wiley Imprint
989 Market Street, San Francisco, CA 94103-1741—www.josseybass.com

Library of Congress Cataloging-in-Publication Data

Keehley, Patricia.
    Benchmarking in the public and nonprofit sectors: best practices for achieving performance breakthroughs/Patricia Keehley, Neil N. Abercrombie.—2nd ed.
        p.   cm.
    ISBN 978-0-7879-9831-8 (cloth)
        1. Total quality management in government—United States.   2. Benchmarking (Management)—United States.   I. Abercrombie, Neil N.   II. Benchmarking for best practices in the public sector.
III. Title.
    JK468.T67B45   2008
    352.3'57—dc22
                                                                                            2008009375

Printed in the United States of America
SECOND EDITION

HB Printing   10 9 8 7 6 5 4 3 2 1

CONTENTS

PART ONE Welcome to Benchmarking

ONE Foundations of Benchmarking   11

TWO Benchmarking and Performance Measures   27

SEVEN Benchmarking in Nonprofits   127

EIGHT Benchmarking in the International Community   147

PART FOUR Benchmarking and Accountability

NINE Benchmarking for Improving Accountability   161

TEN Benchmarking and Performing an Audit   173

FIGURES, TABLES, EXHIBITS, AND WORKSHEETS

FIGURES

TABLES

EXHIBITS

WORKSHEETS

ACKNOWLEDGMENTS

Like most endeavors, this book could not have been completed without considerable help from many people around the globe. The numerous individuals and organizations cited in this book give it a richness that warrants their recognition. Alex Jensen, city manager for Layton City, Utah, agreed early on to our interviews and quickly responded to our follow-up questions. Melanie Hoff of the U.S. Environmental Protection Agency spent time brainstorming the solution-driven methodology with us and provided much needed feedback on how to validate it. Jim Pugh, executive director of the Utah Food Bank Services, generously volunteered time for interviews and observations. We also thank the staff at Discovery Gateway and at the Utah Nonprofits Association, participants in the Utah Benchmarking Project, and staff at Park City Municipal Corporation, all of whom contributed important case study information.

Many of our friends and colleagues associated with the Graduate School, USDA supported us through various projects, including this book, over the past twelve years. Stephen Latimer of the Pacific Islands Training Initiative was particularly patient with all our virtual meetings. Jack Maykoski and Jason Aubuchon were supportive and curious about how we would integrate the Pacific Islands Training Initiative and Virgin Islands Training Initiative projects into the text. Ronnell Rauum and Elaine Muir, also with the Graduate School, USDA, in the Government Audit Training Institute consistently encouraged auditors to be trained on benchmarking. Sharon Barcellos with the Executive Leadership Program of the Graduate School, USDA always had encouraging words, especially as the teams struggled to apply benchmarking to their home organizations. Beyond doubt this book has been greatly enriched by the ongoing work of the energetic and competent staff at the Graduate School, USDA.

We also wish to thank our colleagues at the Utah League of Cities and Towns and Southern Utah University. We particularly appreciated their patience with our monologues about benchmarking. Thanks are also due to Ken Bullock, Lincoln Shurtz, Brian Hall, Sandi Levy, Carl Franklin, and all the others who expressed interest in our endeavor.

Michelle Schmid devoted a considerable amount of time to helping us with the research and final touches to the manuscript. Concurrently, she started an MPA degree program and worked full-time. Many thanks to her for her competent research and her help in tightening the loose ends. Linda Bult polished the draft and provided excellent editorial assistance.

We want to give special thanks to Steve Medlin, Kerri Nakamura, Susan Keehley, Brenda Hancock, and Bill Oakes, who gave life to the chapters on performance measures and solution-driven benchmarking. Their expert training and facilitation in Cambridge, Maryland, brought energy and focus to their respective teams, ultimately providing the excellent examples used in Chapter Five, "The Solution-Driven Benchmarking Method."

And we offer many thanks to our families for their patience with our constant response, "I can't because I'm working on the book." Without the love and support of Cate and Steve and Mica, this book would not exist.

Finally, we greatly appreciate all the contributions from all the individuals and organizations who assisted us, but we are completely responsible for any mistakes or errors in this book.

THE AUTHORS

Patricia Keehley has over thirty years of public, nonprofit, and private sector management and consulting experience. In 1994, she founded iKon Group, inc., which provides training and technical assistance to government and nonprofit organizations throughout the United States and internationally. The lead author of *Benchmarking for Best Practices in the Public Sector*, she serves in the same role for this second edition.

Keehley has trained public and nonprofit employees in benchmarking throughout the United States and internationally, in Egypt, Guam, the Federated States of Micronesia, and Switzerland. Her consulting clients include the Graduate School, USDA; Utah League of Cities and Towns; Colorado Division of Wildlife; Colorado Department of Agriculture; Cedar City Care and Share; and the Southwest Utah Community Health Center. Through her research and consulting she developed the solution-driven method of benchmarking.

Currently, Keehley is assistant professor of political science and director of the Master of Public Administration Program at Southern Utah University in Cedar City, Utah. She has also served on the board of the Summit School District in Colorado and on the planning commission for Cedar City, Utah. She was awarded an MPA degree from the University of South Florida, Tampa, in 1983 and a Ph.D. degree in public administration from the University of Georgia in 1990.

Neil N. Abercrombie is a policy analyst for the Utah League of Cities and Towns. His research focuses on municipal finance, local government management, and municipal government and nonprofit sector collaboration. He is also a member of the Utah Benchmarking Project steering committee; this project is focused on improving the efficiency of municipal government service delivery. He participates in several community nonprofit organizations, including serving as a board member of the Utah Coalition Against Sexual Assault.

He was awarded an MS degree in political science from Utah State University (USU), where he also worked as a graduate research assistant for the USU Institute of Political Economy. He has presented papers at conferences of the Association for Public Policy Analysis and Management and the Western Political Science Association. He is currently working on his dissertation in a doctoral program at the University of Utah, where he is studying public administration and American government, with an emphasis on local government.

Introduction

Why does anyone need a second edition of a book on bench-marking? In a word—technology. Fast-paced communication and economic exchange have revolutionized our world as much as fire changed the caveman's world and electricity ushered in the machine age just a few generations ago. Managers and staff expected technology to make their processes more efficient, but did they expect it to change the way they benchmark or the way they seek and find best practices? Has technology changed the way people adapt those practices to their departments, agencies, and workgroups? What have people learned over the past ten years about how to find benchmarking partners and ways to improve practices? Have they established criteria for best practices? These were our primary questions when we began research for the second edition of this book. We realized quickly that as with most research, initial answers led us at lightning speed to more questions. We were reassured to find that the original benchmarking methodology is still in use and producing good results. And we were delighted to discover a streamlined benchmarking methodology permeating public and nonprofit organizations. We call this new method *solution-driven benchmarking,* because the need to compare and improve is energized by the immediate need to find a solution. You do not need to focus on a process when using solution-driven benchmarking.

Before we go further, let us introduce you to *Benchmarking in the Public and Nonprofit Sectors: Best Practices for Achieving Performance Breakthroughs.* We designed this book to improve the individual and organizational performance of public and nonprofit managers, leaders, staff, and workgroups. If you can't find a way to use this book, let us know. We have found that either the solution-driven approach or the traditional benchmarking approach can be applied to virtually every aspect of public and nonprofit organizations. Moreover, we have found examples of the use of benchmarking in almost every corner of federal, state, and local governments, and benchmarking appears to be widespread among nonprofit organizations as well. We discuss cases from the U.S. Environmental Protection Agency, the Guam Memorial Hospital Authority, the Utah Food Bank, and Layton City, Utah. International cases include Scotland's benchmarking projects with countries such as Costa Rica and South Africa, and in India, Bangalore's benchmarking of footpaths. Each case reconfirms the robust nature of the benchmarking methodology. So sit back, relax with your coffee or tea, and let's get started.

Our book is divided into four parts; each arms the reader with special information designed to enhance an individual's or an organization's performance. Part One, "Welcome to Benchmarking," offers two chapters to help you understand the framework within which we discuss benchmarking. We want you to know that benchmarking has continued to be valuable throughout several significant changes in the way the public sector approaches performance improvement.

Chapter One, "Foundations of Benchmarking," defines benchmarking, places it on a timeline that begins in the early 1980s, and projects it out to 2010. Since our first edition was published, benchmarking has eclipsed total quality management, has sustained its usefulness through reinventing government, and has been embraced by the Government Performance and Results Act of 1993.

Chapter Two, "Benchmarking and Performance Measures," introduces in greater detail the foundation for benchmarking—performance measures. In this chapter we suggest that performance measures must be your partner along the path to improvement. This chapter presents definitions of many performance measurement terms commonly used in the public, private, and nonprofit sectors today. And it explains why you cannot benchmark without performance measures or goals for improvement. It also describes how and why a second benchmarking method took shape and is currently in use across this country.

Once the historical framework and the role of performance measures have been established, we move into methodologies. The introduction to Part Two, "Benchmarking Methods," guides you in selecting the right benchmarking method for you. We highlight the differences between the two methods—traditional and solution driven—and offer criteria for selecting the one more appropriate for various situations.

Chapter Three, "Preparing for Benchmarking," discusses an organization's readiness for benchmarking and provides a few questions you can use to determine that readiness. It also lays out the conceptual differences between the traditional and solution-driven methods and compares the steps in each approach.

We discuss the steps required to complete a traditional benchmarking study in Chapter Four, "The Traditional Benchmarking Method." The traditional methodology has proven to be a very reliable way to compare and improve processes. We offer updated examples from federal, state, and local governments, and we also discuss the benefits and potential challenges found in using the traditional benchmarking approach. We conclude this chapter by explaining how the limitations of the traditional method led to the solution-driven approach.

In Chapter Five, "The Solution-Driven Benchmarking Method," we introduce solution-driven benchmarking. We explain why and how it evolved and distinguish it from simple problem-solving activities. Solution-driven benchmarking is in general use in today's organizations, yet it has gone unrecognized for several years. We present several examples that were developed in a few days by a training class at the Graduate School, U.S. Department of Agriculture (USDA), and we also discuss several case examples from the international and nonprofit communities as well as state and local governments. The solution-driven methodology is sleek, easy to use, and ready for the twenty-first century. We think you will enjoy applying it and find that it yields excellent results.

While writing this book we came to realize the importance of addressing the topic of Part Three, "Benchmarking in Sectors." Here, we feature industry-specific discussions about ways to apply the two methods and follow the examples. Chapter Six, "Benchmarking in State and Local Governments," describes how benchmarking evolved in these government sectors. Many states have used the traditional benchmarking method to improve their agencies. Local governments have a plethora of data to compare, but do they actually benchmark? Absolutely. State and local governments offer numerous promising practices to each other and to the federal and nonprofit sectors. More important, state and local governments have blended the traditional and solution-driven methods in ways that could reveal the next generation of benchmarking methodologies.

Chapter Seven, "Benchmarking in Nonprofits," explores how nonprofit organizations have successfully completed benchmarking projects. We first define nonprofits and explain their unique niche in delivering products and services. Examples in this chapter provide strong evidence that benchmarking is a useful tool that almost guarantees positive results. We believe that the headwaters of solution-driven benchmarking can be found in nonprofits. Lacking substantial resources yet having an urgent need to find best practices, leaders and managers of nonprofit organizations contributed significantly to the solution-driven approach.

Chapter Eight, "Benchmarking in the International Community," reveals when and how other countries are using benchmarking methods to improve performance. Examples from such faraway places as Bangalore, India, and Niger, Scotland, and Costa Rica illustrate what is happening abroad. In many instances the methods used in other countries are remarkably similar to those used in the United States, indicating once again the robustness of benchmarking for finding best practices. We also provide examples from the Guam Memorial Hospital Authority and the Guam Department of Administration to demonstrate how the solution-driven method is used internationally.

In Part Four, "Benchmarking and Accountability," we present two chapters that show how benchmarking assists with accountability. Chapter Nine, "Benchmarking for Improving Accountability," describes several ways that benchmarking can help hold public and nonprofit organizations accountable for performance. When they use benchmarking as a proactive tool, elected and career officials have a constructive way to demonstrate accountability and high performance. We wrote Chapter Ten, "Benchmarking and Performing an Audit," for a special group of people. The practice of auditing has evolved alongside benchmarking, and auditors are in a unique position to encourage organizations to search for best practices. In this chapter we discuss the role of auditors in the benchmarking process and how they can prod agencies into action. Auditors have well-developed research, data collection, and analysis skills, all of which are vital to both benchmarking methods. In this chapter auditors and agencies can learn how they can work together to find and implement promising practices. We also link benchmarking to the elements of a finding and to the audit planning process so that auditors can readily apply benchmarking concepts when conducting an audit.

Chapter Eleven, "Conclusion," reiterates important points and issues. For example, the effort devoted to the benchmarking process should not supersede the outcomes from benchmarking. Similarly, we strongly believe benchmarking should be used to produce positive progress, not punitive actions. Little attention has been devoted to developing a taxonomy of benchmarking studies or to evaluating the long-term success of best practices. If we have convinced you to use one or both of the benchmarking methods, we want to give you a good start. We conclude this chapter with a discussion about the future of benchmarking.

When you are looking for specific information about benchmarking methods, Table I.1 will help you find the chapters you need. You may also use Worksheet I.1, in the Resources section in the back of the book, for finding and recording answers to specific questions.

Table I.1
What Are You Looking For?

When You're Looking For . . .	Try Looking Here
Context and history	Chapter One: "Foundations of Benchmarking"
Relationship between training and benchmarking	Chapter One: "Foundations of Benchmarking"
Concepts in and uses of performance measures	Chapter Two: "Benchmarking and Performance Measures"
Relationship between performance measures and benchmarking	Chapter Two: "Benchmarking and Performance Measures"
Comparisons and conceptual differences between the methods	Chapter Three: "Preparing for Benchmarking"

(Continued)

Table I.1 (Continued)

When You're Looking For . . .	Try Looking Here
How to select a method	Chapter Three: "Preparing for Benchmarking"
Examples and instructions for using traditional benchmarking	Chapter Four: "The Traditional Benchmarking Method"
Examples and instructions for using solution-driven benchmarking	Chapter Five: "The Solution-Driven Benchmarking Method"
Cases of benchmarking at state and local government levels	Chapter Six: "Benchmarking in State and Local Governments"
Cases of benchmarking in nonprofits	Chapter Seven: "Benchmarking in Nonprofits"
Cases of benchmarking throughout the world	Chapter Eight: "Benchmarking in the International Community"
Ways that benchmarking can help accountability	Chapter Nine: "Benchmarking for Improving Accountability"
Ways that auditors can use benchmarking	Chapter Ten: "Benchmarking and Performing an Audit"
How elements of a finding link to the benchmarking steps	Chapter Ten: "Benchmarking and Performing an Audit"
Areas that need additional research	Chapter Eleven: "Conclusion"
Quick, easy steps to launch your benchmarking project	Chapter Eleven: "Conclusion"
Worksheets, including checklists, to get you started and help you complete the benchmarking process	Resources
Definitions of terms	Glossary
More help in finding things	Index

In addition to the chapters we have just described, we have provided a glossary in the back of the book. Throughout the past fifteen years we have been repeatedly frustrated with the misuse of performance measurement and benchmarking terms. We want to ensure that you have a clear understanding of how we use these terms, and we encourage you to adopt these definitions as your own.

This book was written with the practitioner in mind, and so we have also included a resource that contains numerous worksheets to help you negotiate any benchmarking activity.

Finally, we hope you enjoy the book and find it useful. We also offer a password-protected Instructor's Guide online at www.wiley.com/college/keehley. The Instructor's Guide lays out a two-day workshop that can be delivered by an instructor with benchmarking experience. This workshop offers any organization the opportunity to train benchmarking teams on the concepts, tools, and techniques necessary for a successful benchmarking study. The worksheets found in this text are integrated into the workshop. We will gladly assist the instructor or teams if you or they have questions or would like additional information.

It is our sincere hope that you enjoy this book and find it useful.

PART ONE

Welcome to Benchmarking

Before jumping into a benchmarking project it is important to understand how benchmarking evolved into a methodology and some of the cornerstones in its foundation. Chapter One, "Foundations of Benchmarking," provides basic definitions of *benchmark* and *benchmarking*. It also describes how benchmarking evolved from a process developed at the Xerox Corporation into a method commonly and widely used throughout the United States and internationally. Benchmarking has remained a stable and reliable methodology through several decades and various performance improvement trends. In Chapter One we also discuss the definition of *best practice* and offer a new term, *promising practice,* that can be used interchangeably.

In Chapter Two, "Benchmarking and Performance Measures," we introduce several conceptual models to help benchmarking teams understand the basics of performance measures. Benchmarking is inextricably linked to measurements because a baseline, or starting point, for performance must be established from which comparisons can be made. Measures are also critical to demonstrating that a best practice has had a positive impact on performance. We provide numerous examples and illustrations to help anyone interested in benchmarking to get started.

Foundations of Benchmarking

The term *benchmark* has had important, practical applications from its earliest use. The first stone laid at the ground level for a medieval castle was the benchmark upon which all other stones were oriented. Similarly, a significant rock or stone in a large parcel of land was a benchmark, the point from which the land was measured and divided. In those days your cobbler marked a notch in his bench as a point of reference for your shoe size. So *benchmark* can be defined as a point of comparison and used interchangeably with the word *standard.* In short, the use of the word has changed very little from the Middle Ages to the twenty-first century.

> *A benchmark is a standard or point of comparison.*

Benchmarking is the process of comparing one organization's process to another's in an attempt to discover best practices that, once imported, will improve operations. The traditional approach to this process is rooted in the private sector. One of the most frequently cited private sector cases is the benchmarking project conducted by Xerox with L.L. Bean in the early 1980s. Although they are very different companies, Xerox learned important lessons from L.L. Bean about warehouse management and distribution. We modified the definition provided in the first edition to a more concise version.

Benchmarking is a methodology used to improve performance by finding high-performing organizations and importing their practices to the home organization.

This private sector tool was quickly adopted by the public and nonprofit sectors in the late 1980s and early 1990s. The search for best practices traditionally requires an organization to follow a series of well-defined steps. Benchmarking is largely a technical method and can be a powerful tool for improving organizational performance. Like any other approach or methodology, a benchmarking project needs to fit within and support the goals, objectives, vision, and strategic plan of the agency in which it is used.

HISTORICAL CONTEXT
The First Wave: Total Quality Management

During the 1980s, U.S. managers quietly began borrowing a performance improvement movement called *total quality management* (TQM) from Japanese companies and inserting it into industries in the United States (Ghobadian & Speller, 1994). Originally developed in the 1950s by an American, W. Edwards Deming, TQM was all about improving profits and reducing errors by analyzing and changing processes. Deming and Joseph M. Juran, another expert in quality improvement, worked to help Japanese industries rebuild after World War II. Most U.S. companies ignored Deming, Juran, and TQM until their profit margins fell and until it became widely known that the quality of Japanese products was becoming better than that of U.S. products. American companies had to become more competitive. They began to adopt TQM principles and practices in hopes of regaining their competitive edge.

In the late 1970s and early 1980s, Xerox adopted a TQM approach and began comparing its operations in the northwest United States with similar Xerox operations around the world (Camp, 1998). Xerox used teams that evaluated their organization's work processes, visited other locations, identified practices with potential for improving process performance, and then adapted the practices to their home location. This series of steps, which included complex analyses and significant organizational changes, needed a short name. It was a small, albeit, important component of total quality management—a systematic way of measuring a process, finding similar processes to use as comparisons, and then importing process steps as necessary to become more efficient and reduce costs. Comparisons were made with organizations that were performing better on selected metrics than the home organization was. These better performing organizations came to be known as *partners,* regardless of the degree of effort expended by them in this process. In most instances the partner was helpful and cooperative. The process changes imported to improve performance came to be known as *best practices.* And the overall method of improving process performance by finding partners with best practices became known as *benchmarking.*

The Xerox benchmarking methodology has been replicated and altered somewhat but remains essentially the same. In most instances a benchmarking study begins with a team charter. Individuals drawn from various organizational subunits come together with a mandate to clearly define the problem, the process, and the performance measures. The team members frequently receive training on how to conduct a benchmarking study and how to define and analyze processes. Once the process is defined, the team collects data on process performance and begins to search for benchmarking partners. Benchmarking partners are usually similar organizations that are performing the process better than the benchmarking organization is. The team inquires whether the partner is willing to assist the benchmarking organization. If so, the partner hosts a visit and shares information, and the benchmarking team returns home armed with best practices. *Best practices* are policies, procedures, activities, or operations that lead to high performance. The benchmarking team usually creates an implementation plan to adapt each best practice to the team's organization and monitors performance to ensure that each practice has a positive impact. Here is a generic outline of these common steps. (The chapters in Part Two discuss our more detailed set of eleven steps at length.)

Common Benchmarking Steps

1. Charter and train a team to conduct a benchmarking study.

2. Define the process for benchmarking.

3. Research potential partners.

4. Collect and analyze data.

5. Identify the causes of performance differences.

6. Adapt the high-performing practice(s) to the benchmarking organization.

7. Implement the practice(s) and monitor changes.

Total quality management successes and benchmarking became widely publicized, and private sector organizations quickly adopted TQM and benchmarking as methods to improve performance. Initially, improved performance was defined by the private sector as reduced errors or costs, increased profit margins, or increased market share. These performance indicators changed when benchmarking was applied in the public sector. It was during this period that organizations were introduced to the phrase *best practice*. All benchmarking teams were searching for best practices—things your partner organization did to enhance performance that you had not yet done. A *benchmarking study* was completed to find and import these best practices. Total quality management, benchmarking, and best practices spread like wildfire.

Next the Baldrige Award entered the picture. Established by the U.S. Department of Commerce, the Malcolm Baldrige National Quality Award became a coveted prize (Baldrige National Quality Program, National Institute of Standards and Technology, 2007). Initially, it was given only to private sector companies that clearly demonstrated they had, among other things, streamlined their processes through team efforts and benchmarking. An elaborate evaluation system was developed, and companies spent thousands if not millions of dollars to win the Baldrige. After all, it meant serious recognition among peers and the public for good, efficient management practices. Florida Power won the award in 1989, but only after it spent millions to do so, and its success was later questioned when news of layoffs and customer dissatisfaction hit the press. A few other warts associated with TQM were also starting to show. Nonetheless, TQM and the Baldrige Award received much attention from academics, practitioners, and corporations around the world—and the award continues today. (More information can be found at www.quality.nist.gov.)

Once recognized, Baldrige winners were required to host benchmarking teams from other companies. The idea of benchmarking an organization outside your specific business or industry became fashionable. Proprietary information was guarded, but companies such as L.L. Bean, Xerox, and Motorola opened their doors to benchmarking teams from other companies. Books were written that documented the millions of dollars saved by streamlining processes through quality management and benchmarking. Once the private sector became completely enthralled with quality management and benchmarking, the public sector was quick to jump on board. By 1988, the Baldrige Award was open to public organizations as well.

The Federal Quality Institute (FQI) was created in 1988 to promote TQM and process improvement throughout the federal government. It was staffed primarily by federal employees who were temporarily assigned, or detailed, to FQI from their home agencies. FQI staff provided training and consulting services to federal agencies in TQM, team processes, benchmarking, the Baldrige Award, and other TQM-related activities. The FQI also decided which federal agencies would receive the coveted President's Award for performance improvement. Unfortunately, TQM began to fade, the staff dispersed, and FQI merged into the U.S. Office of Personnel Management. Despite its many successes, TQM came to be seen as another management fad inflicted on career public servants by elected officials. TQM didn't fail; it was simply replaced.

Another Trend: Reinventing Government

President Clinton entered office with a goal of reducing the size of the federal government. Shortly after the inauguration in 1993, Clinton's vice president, Al Gore, was tasked with *reinventing government.* As part of this effort he created the National Partnership for Reinventing Government (2001). Hence, as TQM was fading out, reinvention was rolling in. Reinventing government became the new call to action (Osborne & Gaebler, 1992). Leaders were expected to focus on customers and to question and reframe significant policies and procedures. Reinvention teams replaced process improvement teams. Teams were granted more latitude in their projects. Reinvention activities were not restricted to examining work processes, which was the focus of TQM and benchmarking. Cities such as Sunnyvale, California, were used as examples of how the public sector could *reinvent* itself and improve.

The interest in benchmarking and comparing performance continued through the reinvention era. Government agencies were now actively seeking comparisons in hopes of finding ways to improve. Improvement efforts tended to focus on reduced costs and improved customer satisfaction—that is, on doing more with less. The term *best practice* was used more frequently than ever to describe something that should be tried in the effort to improve.

The benchmarking methodology survived intact through the transition from TQM to reinvention because it was a rock-solid tool that could be used to find ways to improve. No politics required, no organizational culture change—just the application of a reliable method to find a better way to do work. Benchmarking

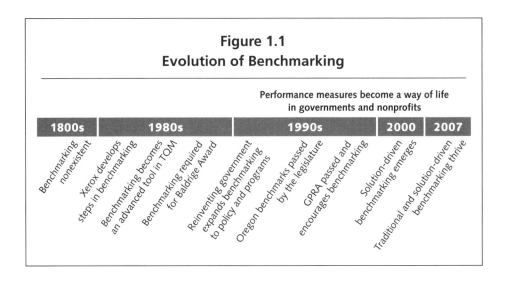

Figure 1.1
Evolution of Benchmarking

Performance measures become a way of life in governments and nonprofits

1800s	1980s	1990s	2000	2007

Benchmarking nonexistent

Xerox develops steps in benchmarking

Benchmarking becomes an advanced tool in TQM

Benchmarking required for Baldrige Award

Reinventing government expands benchmarking to policy and programs

Oregon benchmarks passed by the legislature

GPRA passed and encourages benchmarking

Solution-driven benchmarking emerges

Traditional and solution-driven benchmarking thrive

was also to survive another stage in the evolution of public sector performance improvement (see Figure 1.1).

Like TQM, reinventing government resulted in many improvements in government operations. But government is also about politics. The Clinton administration departed, and efforts to improve performance and reduce costs manifested themselves elsewhere.

Legislating Performance Improvement

The passage of the Government Performance and Results Act (GPRA) in 1993 clearly demonstrated that elected officials wanted the government's delivery of products and services to improve. It was the first time that public officials had legislated a strategic approach to administering government. One of the first GPRA requirements federal departments and agencies had to meet was the development of a strategic plan. They were allowed several years to develop and refine this strategic plan. Then they were required to align their performance measures with their plan. Finally, departments and agencies were expected to report on their strategic plans, performance measures, and improvements by the 2003 budget cycle. The U.S. Office of Management and Budget (OMB) suggested that benchmarking was a good way for federal agencies to find better ways of operating.

Today benchmarking is alive and well throughout federal, state, and local governments and nonprofit organizations (NGOs). But what form of benchmarking has emerged?

BENCHMARKING IN THE TWENTY-FIRST CENTURY

Benchmarking has survived the past couple of decades and several performance improvement trends, but will it continue to serve public and nonprofit organizations by leading them to enhanced performance? The answer is absolutely yes, and here are four reasons why benchmarking is here to stay.

First, the original 1980s benchmarking methodology has evolved into two distinct methods; either one reliably leads the user to a best practice. Having two methods gives users more tools and options for searching for best practices. Second, benchmarking is no longer the domain of a few individuals in each organization who have a passion for finding ways to improve. Numerous and varied public, private, and nonprofit organizations have integrated benchmarking methods into their regular training programs. With so many people trained to use these methods and given the results they yield, the methods are certain to be used repeatedly in the future. Third, the language of performance improvement has permeated public and nonprofit culture. The terms *benchmarking, best practice,* and *performance measure* are commonly used and widely understood. Finally, advances in technology have decreased many previous barriers to collecting and sharing information. The use of Internet, e-mail, and Web 2.0 technology has created bridges between many organizations and created more opportunities for benchmarking.

Indeed, now that organizations are armed with two methodologies, with workforces that have a substantial benchmark-trained component, and with workers who are familiar with benchmarking verbiage from their day-to-day work lives while also benefiting from the fast advances in technology, it is clear that organizations will continue to use benchmarking as a tool well into the twenty-first century.

Two Benchmarking Methodologies

The first benchmarking method—the multistep methodology that originated in the 1980s—has changed very little over the past two decades. Teams are still chartered to examine work processes through flowcharts, data collection and analysis, and comparisons to other organizations. Partners are coveted for their best practices. It is roughly a six-month, resource-intensive process that, when followed closely, virtually guarantees performance improvements. Benchmarking in this form is likely to continue into future decades. We call it *traditional benchmarking*.

The second benchmarking method emerged in the late 1990s and is still evolving. Many government entities have not had the staff or financial resources to pursue a traditional benchmarking study, yet leaders and managers have been motivated to improve, especially with the passage and implementation of the GPRA. Nonprofits and nongovernmental organizations have been in a particularly difficult position in regard to benchmarking because they often have less reliable and potentially more restrictive funding than other organizations do (Poister, 2003). Nonprofits are frequently smaller than federal or state government agencies and depend significantly on grants or contributions for their operating budgets. Often these grants or contributions are specifically intended for service delivery programs, not administrative costs. As a result many nonprofit organizations cannot afford to use the traditional benchmarking method, so an alternative has emerged. Alongside nonprofits, small public agencies such as local governments have also been stressed for funds yet have needed to improve performance.

Fortunately, the traditional benchmarking method had convinced most managers that comparing processes and results and finding the reasons for performance differences could yield important information about ways to improve. The notion that one should "steal shamelessly" any great ideas on how to improve dates back to Deming and Juran and had survived several decades. So the idea of reaching out to others had become wholly acceptable. The idea of importing practices found to be helpful to performance had also become common. It was well embedded in governments, nonprofits, professional associations, and award programs. With that continuing foundation and with so much information available on the Internet, managers began to ask, "Why bother with a six-month examination of a process that may or may not be the primary source of the problem?"

In response to that question, NGOs and small governments refined the traditional benchmarking approach. They began with the greatest problem or pressure point and immediately looked for help. No teams, no charters—just problems, an energetic focus on solutions, a network of professionals, and information available on speed dial or at a keystroke. A food bank facing a fiscal crisis due to increased gas prices cannot spend time chartering a team to examine how to streamline the transportation process. It must act quickly or some food may not be distributed to needy recipients. The *problem at hand* became the driving force behind comparisons—not the *process performance*. Many nonprofits share problems; it was only natural that they share solutions. Thus the *solution-driven benchmarking* method hatched.

Advances in technology have facilitated this new, solution-driven approach. For example, with so much information available on the Internet, why bother with a six-month examination of a process that may or may not be the primary source of the problem? It is now common practice for many managers or staff administrators to begin a search for a solution via Google. They must always ask themselves, however, whether this advanced sharing of ideas and information is really producing best practices.

As this new benchmarking methodology emerged, it became a focus of our research and study for this book. We first identified four major steps commonly used in the solution-driven benchmarking method and then added a fifth step: monitor progress. Continuous improvement is absolutely essential to benchmarking, so managers must monitor progress to verify that a promising practice has actually improved performance.

Solution-Driven Benchmarking Steps

1. Discover the problem.
2. Establish criteria for solutions.
3. Search for promising practices.
4. Implement promising practices.
5. Monitor progress.

Using the solution-driven approach, you are not dependent on a team nor necessarily focused on a process. Hence it is quite different from the traditional method, and we explain it in detail in Chapter Five.

A Workforce Trained on Benchmarking

After several months of research we realized that many of the cases we were presenting in this book were directly related to training activities. The U.S. Environmental Protection Agency, for example, launched its Superfund benchmarking project by training team members.

Moreover, our examples of both the traditional and solution-driven methods are derived from products developed during the Graduate School, USDA executive development programs. These graduate school programs are designed to prepare federal line staff, supervisors, and managers with tools for more effective management. Throughout the programs they devote hours to benchmarking and performance improvement. Hence an enormous variety of federal employees have a working knowledge of benchmarking.

An example is the case of the U.S. Department of the Interior (DOI) auditor general who became a strong advocate of including best practices in audit reports. To prepare his staff he mandated that all DOI Office of Inspector General (OIG) auditors receive training on how to benchmark. This gave those of us who provided the training and the training participants an opportunity to discuss and explore their role in the benchmarking process, and what we learned is directly linked to how we developed the auditor's role in benchmarking.

Benchmarking is very effective in other kinds of training sessions as well. For example, in 2007, Guam Memorial Hospital Authority (GMHA) staff participated in a two-week training session on workload analysis. During those two weeks they spent some time learning how to use the solution-driven method to find best practices. We discuss their success in Chapter Five, "The Solution-Driven Benchmarking Method."

Also, the U.S. government provides considerable financial support for training representatives from developing countries on how to benchmark. For example, the U.S. Agency for International Development funded a benchmarking partnership between cities in Bulgaria and Golden, Colorado (Henderson, 2007). This partnership was part of larger development and improvement projects, and training on how to conduct a benchmarking study can also be effective as part of broader efforts to improve operations and performance, as it was when the DOI Office of Insular Affairs funded training on performance improvement and benchmarking for GMHA and other Pacific island government agencies.

As part of our senior-level education and training programs, the Graduate School, USDA provides hands-on benchmarking experiences for public employees with other agencies as well as private industry. This experience has proven to be a valuable tool for program participants to apply to their organizations.

**—Sharon Barcellos, senior program manager,
Center for Leadership and Management, Graduate School,
USDA (personal communication, March 2007)**

Our research has led us to an important conclusion—training can greatly enhance the benchmarking experience. We encourage anyone or any group that is ready to launch a benchmarking project to invest in training. The cost can range from minimal (the price of this book, for example) to extensive (the cost of hiring outside consultants to train your workforce and guide the entire process). Select the level of support most appropriate for your organization, but do get some support. Without a doubt, benchmark training is a tool you can use in tandem with benchmarking to find and import best practices.

Changing Attitudes Toward Best Practices

The title of our first edition was *Benchmarking for Best Practices in the Public Sector.* At the time that book was written, the term *best practice* was fairly new. A best practice was an exciting discovery, one that helped an organization to perform better. In our first edition we stressed that an organization should establish criteria when it begins searching for a best practice. We raised several questions about how best practices should be defined. We warned against overzealously calling everything a best practice. We suggested being wary and somewhat suspicious when someone reported a best practice, and seeking proof before accepting it as such. In this edition we completely reverse this opinion.

Since the early 1980s, the purpose of benchmarking has been to find the best practice embedded in a partner's organization and to import it to one's home organization. A best practice has represented a positive activity—something good the benchmarking team has found elsewhere that it wants to try. In the past when public organizations claimed they had found a best practice, practitioners listened and assumed it would be good. The National Conference of Mayors, for example, asked its members to submit their best practices and published the resulting list with no questions asked. No method was applied to evaluate the practices. Similarly, when Phoenix, Arizona, discovered privatization of garbage collection, it was declared a best practice for all cities. It turned out that this practice could be a disaster under some circumstances. In the 1990s, no one seemed to recognize the need to be cautious when promoting a best practice. What has changed?

Although we still find simple assertions that some things are best practices a bit disconcerting, this is much less worrisome than it was in the 1990s. Why? Everyone got smarter about it. It took only a few instances like the Phoenix case and numerous lists of untested best practices before organizations became cautious and much less likely to rush to import a best practice. And some organizations and groups continue to raise questions about the usefulness of the term itself. For example, Anne Richards, the DOI's assistant auditor general, spearheaded the benchmarking training for the auditors on her staff. As we designed the training, she indicated a reluctance to use the phrase *best practice*. By using *promising practice* instead, the audit staff introduced a bit of caution, suggesting that a practice had potential but was not yet considered a best practice. We like this phrase, and we use it where appropriate in this book. We cannot, however, avoid using *best practice*, because that term has permeated our performance improvement language. A simple search through Google on *best practice* yields thousands of links, ranging from peacekeeping best practices of the United Nations to the best way to stop e-mail spam. The universal use of the term is obvious.

> *A best practice or promising practice is an idea, practice, process step, or policy that will improve performance in the organization that adopts it.*

Sources of Best Practices

No matter which benchmarking methodology you choose, you are looking for a best or promising practice. Consider three sources of best and promising practices and whether each source is appropriate for your organization.

A Best Practice Is Self-Declared   When practitioners learn about new ideas or practices, they frequently refer to these discoveries as *best practices*. The popularity of this term and people's comfort with it make it easy to use and suggest that there really is a *best* way of doing things. But the term is relative and its meaning can depend on the individual or the organization that has discovered or claims it. So judging an idea by its label alone has some dangers. If you are looking for a best practice for your organization, be sure that you determine who declared it a best practice and examine the evidence that demonstrates that it is. The fact that a practice is different from your own practice and appears to work for others does not make it a best practice, nor does it guarantee that the practice will work for you.

Wayne Welsh, CPA with the Utah Office of Legislative Auditor General, prepared a report titled *Best Practices for Good Management* (Office of Legislative Auditor General & Welsh, 2000–2001). In it he declares several best practices, such as develop a strategic plan, prioritize goals, identify stakeholders, and develop a mission statement. These practices are no doubt important to follow and may be among the top five or ten of the most important management practices. This list could probably be found in many management books, and we agree they are good management practices. But you do not need benchmarking to find them.

Emerging Industry Trends Can Be a Source of Best Practices   In 1993, the report of the National Performance Review, by Al Gore, recommended that a variety of best practices be adopted by the federal government, including the use of high-speed networks, electronic benefits transfer, and public access to online data. Although managers today take them for granted, at the time these were cutting-edge trends and ideas that were emerging from the private sector. In retrospect, these were great ideas and virtually all levels of government have implemented them.

Most recently, the public sector has been adopting some of the practices created in the private sector to take advantage of Web 2.0 advances. Web 2.0 is a second generation of online communication. This latest Internet wave features a number of new ways for individuals to share information and create online communities (blogs, podcasts, MySpace, Facebook, wikis, and so on). One example of the public sector embracing this movement is the creation of wikis. The popularity of Wikipedia, where anyone can create an account and contribute or revise encyclopedia-type entries, has inspired new modes of communication for some local governments. Davis, California, for instance, has created the DavisWiki, an online community where individuals can "explore, discuss, and compile anything and everything about Davis, California" (DavisWiki, 2007). The objective of making everyone eligible to contribute to, add to, or revise the Web site was to go beyond personal blogs and create, in essence, a blog for the entire community.

Conversely, in the 1990s, performance-based budgeting (PBB) was (some would argue it still is) a public sector trend assumed to be a best practice that would help communities hold public organizations accountable for performance. The road to implementing PBB has been long and difficult, although some governments have been successful in traversing it. PBB was an industry trend that was apparently not right for everyone.

A Best Practice Is an Award-Winning Success   Perhaps the most reliable sources of promising practices are the numerous award and recognition programs. Many professional associations and universities have established best practice award programs or databases. Organization members, or in some cases the public, can search these materials on line to find promising practices for almost every aspect of public sector management.

The best practices identified by award programs appear more reliable than the lists of best practices gathered from organization members do because the awards program practices have been evaluated. The International City/County Management Association (ICMA), for example, annually evaluates submissions, consistently applying criteria that help to ensure the practices are safe for others to follow.

Another example is the Carl Bertelsmann Prize for the best-managed city. In 1993, the competition was based on performance in customer service, employee involvement, planning, innovation, and bureaucratic downsizing (Kwok, 1993, p. A1). The prize recognizes municipalities that have innovatively adjusted their structure and operations to meet challenges and that have overcome their traditional authority model. The award is also designed to encourage other cities to begin their own transformation (Bertelsmann-Stiftung, 2004).

Similarly, the Performance Institute has established a best practices database. The institute states it is backed by a national research base on best management practices in government. The ICMA has established a Center for Performance Measurement that compiles information about best practices among program participants.

Make no mistake, we strongly believe that thousands of public organizations have benefited by importing practices discovered at other organizations. But we reiterate that all organizations should closely examine whether using a relativistic definition of best practice can put an organization in the risky position of importing *ideas,* not practices, which ultimately may cause more harm than good. The risk is that too many unproven ideas will be tried and that precious dollars will be wasted in areas that produce minimal fiscal returns.

SUMMARY

- A benchmark is a standard or point of comparison.
- Benchmarking is a methodology used to find best or promising practices.
- The benchmarking methodology has remained consistent through numerous performance improvement trends. We refer to this as *traditional benchmarking.*

- Traditional benchmarking is completed by a team that defines and analyzes a process, searches for best practices through partner organizations, adapts and imports the practice, and monitors long-term implementation to ensure success.

- Solution-driven benchmarking can be completed by individuals or small teams who define the problem, search for solutions through professional networks and the Internet, import the practice, and monitor short-term changes.

- Many public and nonprofit staff, managers, and leaders have been trained in how to benchmark. A widely trained workforce is likely to sustain benchmarking into the future.

- The term *best practices* has become part of organizations' day-to-day language. We use it, along with *promising practices,* in reference to an idea, practice, process step, or policy that will improve performance in the organization that adopts it.

You may also use Worksheet 1.1, in the Resources, for reviewing this chapter.

Benchmarking and Performance Measures

The secretary of education for the government of Yap, a small island in the Pacific, once expressed a serious concern with performance measures. Yap receives a considerable amount of funding from the U.S. government, and the U.S. Department of Education was requiring Yap to collect and report performance measures. The Yap secretary explained that U.S. measures are fixed. They cannot change or be flexible. He stretched out his arms and said, "To us, this is a fathom. To the U.S. a fathom is always six feet." When the Yapese discuss a fathom, they recognize that the length varies depending on the arm span of the speaker. The secretary was baffled by the U.S. expectation that his department could collect and report measures that were fixed and always represented the same amount. This confusion was complicated by the Yapese language. In the English language and culture the numbers one, one hundred, and one thousand are stable and can be consistently applied to anything that can be counted. But in Yapese and several other languages spoken in the Pacific islands, different words are used for the same number, depending on what is being counted. Fish, for example, are counted differently from trees. Imposing performance measurement requirements on these governments and cultures creates opportunities for some interesting discussions.

PURPOSE OF PERFORMANCE MEASURES

Every organization is formed and exists to accomplish a purpose, and that purpose drives its daily operations. The purpose of a public or nonprofit organization is not always as straightforward or as clear as the purpose of a private (or for-profit) sector organization. Public and nonprofit organizations may be created for many purposes, sometimes even competing purposes. For example, one purpose of a municipality is to encourage business development. Yet another purpose, which may compete with business development, is to ensure that businesses comply with licensing and operating requirements. One purpose of a police department is to ensure the safety of citizens. A school district's purpose is to educate students. A hospital exists to restore the health of sick or injured patients. A professional association provides its members with timely information and services related to the profession and professional development.

A simple model illustrates how public and nonprofit organizations *measure,* or link their strategic purpose to their day-to-day operations. This model has four components: outcomes, outputs, process, and inputs. To define each component of the model, ask the following questions:

Outcomes	What is the organization's purpose?
	What does the organization hope that linking operations will ultimately accomplish?
	What are the strategic goals?
Outputs	What products or services are delivered on a regular basis to customers or constituents?
Process	What work steps or activities are completed that result in the delivery of products or services?
Inputs	What money is spent on salaries or other expenses to ensure that the process is completed and that the products or services are delivered?

Outcomes

Think about your organization (agency, department, or nonprofit group, for example). What is its primary purpose or reason for existing? What is it trying to accomplish? What are its strategic goals? When these questions have been answered, the organization's desired *outcomes* have been identified. All organizations have at least one desired outcome, and most have several. Sure, the police department exists to ensure the safety of its citizens, but it also exists to identify those who break the law. Hospitals restore the health of patients in the emergency room, but they also serve the community at large by providing laboratory services and facilities for elective surgery. The outcomes are frequently articulated in the organization's strategic plan, typically in the form of broad goals to be achieved over a relatively long period of time (about five years).

Outputs

Products or services delivered are called *outputs*. Organizations assume that if enough of the right outputs are generated over a period of time, they will achieve their outcomes. Most organizations do not instantly achieve their outcomes. Hospitals cannot instantly restore health to everyone in the emergency room. Police cannot build a wall of safety around every citizen. Libraries cannot deliver all needed information to every household in the area. But by delivering products and services on a day-to-day basis, organizations hope to accomplish long-term outcomes.

An organization's outputs can be discovered by asking one question: "What does this organization provide directly to a citizen or constituent?" In some cases multiple products or services are provided by a single organization. The U.S. Internal Revenue Service (IRS) collects taxes, answers taxpayers' questions, and issues refund checks. A state department of transportation builds and repairs roads and issues weather and road condition warnings. Police departments answer 911 calls, arrest criminals, and issue tickets for traffic violations. A library allows citizens to borrow books, use reference materials, and access the Internet. All of these are outputs because each describes a product or service delivered by the organization.

Public and nonprofit organizations often struggle to determine which outputs they should deliver because it is unclear whether a certain output actually results in the desired outcome. Arresting criminals is an excellent output, but will it lead to improved citizen safety? Possibly, but maybe not. When economic conditions are extremely poor, citizens with no criminal history may turn to crime, but arresting them may not affect citizens' overall safety. Treating a heart attack patient in a hospital is an output, but an emergency room generally does nothing to address ongoing prevention or treatment of heart disease.

With limited resources, all public and nonprofit organizations are forced to limit outputs to those they determine are most likely (or proven) to lead to the desired outcomes.

Process

Public and nonprofit entities must organize and energize staff and physical resources to produce outputs. Human resources, computers, telephones, equipment, and all the other things that make up an organization's operations are organized (sometimes inefficiently) in a way that leads to the production of a product or service. The activities or work steps taken to generate the product or service are, collectively, called a *process*. Staff apply themselves to this process and use tools such as computers, paper, pens, telephones, desks, elevators, fax machines, and all the other paraphernalia found in offices and other work areas to assist them. Organizations have established rules, policies, and procedures to ensure that the process operates smoothly and that only those entitled to the product or service actually receive it. A police officer might complete the following process as part of arresting a person driving under the influence of alcohol:

1. Observe a swerving automobile.

2. Signal the driver to pull over.

3. Assess the driver's condition by administering a breathalyzer test.

4. Impound the driver's car.

5. Formalize the arrest, and take the driver to jail.

A librarian is likely to complete this process when checking out books for a patron:

1. Request a library card.

2. Scan the library card.

3. Scan the books.

4. Print a receipt with the required return date.

5. Disarm a magnetic alarm.

6. Hand the books and the receipt to the customer.

Inputs

Public and nonprofit organizations must pay employee salaries and purchase supplies and equipment as part of supporting the process and delivering the product or service. Where does the money come from to purchase these things? Each year public or nonprofit organizations receive money from such sources as appropriations, revenues, fees, grants, or other sources. These funds are considered *inputs* to an organization. In most cases they are spent with the intention that the organization will deliver outputs that result in the desired outcome.

Ideally, when a public or nonprofit organization is first created or when it is reevaluating or reconfirming its purpose, it develops a strategic plan. The strategic plan typically begins by defining the desired outcomes or strategic goals. The outputs, process, and inputs should be aligned with and should function in support of these outcomes although this is a very difficult task indeed. The model presented in Figure 2.1 is a great conceptual illustration of the relationship between an organization's strategies and daily operations. Note that the model does not represent what happens during actual process execution (which occurs in the reverse order).

IPOLO Model of Operations

A more practical model for linking an organization's strategies to daily operations has almost identical components but in reverse order. IPOLO is an acronym for inputs, process, outputs, link, and outcomes (Figure 2.2). Organizations do not begin each day with staff asking, "What is our purpose," or, "What are we trying to accomplish in the long run?" Quite the opposite happens. Each day, funding (inputs) is used to purchase labor and equipment that are combined into work steps, activities, or functions (that is, into a process). The work process leads to

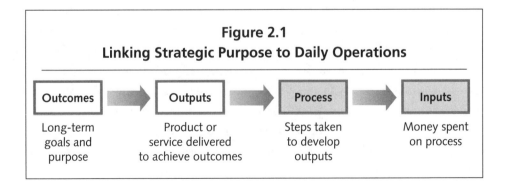

Figure 2.1
Linking Strategic Purpose to Daily Operations

Outcomes	Outputs	Process	Inputs
Long-term goals and purpose	Product or service delivered to achieve outcomes	Steps taken to develop outputs	Money spent on process

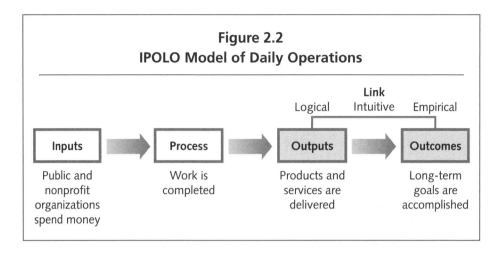

Figure 2.2
IPOLO Model of Daily Operations

Inputs	Process	Outputs	Outcomes
Public and nonprofit organizations spend money	Work is completed	Products and services are delivered	Long-term goals are accomplished

Link
Logical Intuitive Empirical

the delivery of products or services (outputs). For example, a hospital hires physicians and nurses to treat patients. A school system hires teachers to teach students. Police departments hire officers to patrol streets and arrest criminals. Ultimately, the outputs lead to the desired outcomes of healthy citizens, citizens with a good education, and safe neighborhoods. The flow from inputs to process to outputs and to outcomes is an ideal model to apply to the repeated operations of public or nonprofit organizations.

In addition to the inputs, process, outputs, and outcomes also found in our first model, the IPOLO model displays a link between outputs and outcomes. This indicates that a logical, intuitive, or empirical link must exist between the outputs and outcomes. The link helps justify the money spent on the process to deliver products and services. As a taxpayer you should be expected to fund only those outputs that lead to desired outcomes. A cause-and-effect relationship should exist, but it is often very difficult to prove. For example, one output of airport security is passengers clearing security. When passengers are cleared on a daily basis, are airports more secure? The answer is yes if you believe terrorists have been discouraged by increased passenger screening. The answer is no if you believe terrorists find ways around passenger screening. Despite many people's best efforts, the relationship between passenger screenings and increased security is unproven. Similarly, environmental agencies inspect for hazardous waste at manufacturing plants and issue citations or fines when violations occur. The outputs (citations and fines) presumably deter and punish in a way that motivates the manufacturer to comply. But the relationship between citations, fines, and compliance is arguable.

Public and nonprofit organizations do their very best to link the outputs and outcomes and should be held accountable for doing so. We suggest that organizations ensure that a logical, intuitive, or empirical link between outputs and outcomes exists and that the link be periodically checked. If the link cannot be demonstrated or supported over time, the organization should reconsider the outputs. Money should be redirected toward a process that results in different outputs. For example, the No Child Left Behind Act has been widely criticized for its emphasis on testing. The Act's desired outcome was to improve public education. Federal funds were provided for school systems to test students (outputs). Some now argue that testing students led to improved education because test scores increased. Others argue that test scores indicate that students only learn how to perform on the test and that their overall education in fact declined. School districts spent money on processes to enhance test scores and sometimes eliminated subjects not covered on the test, such as physical education. The federal government redirected funds to states and schools whose outputs (test scores) improved. The redirecting of money to these schools illustrates the relationship between long-term goals, outputs, and funding. But the overall example also illustrates the difficulty of linking outputs to outcomes.

A link is a logical, intuitive, or empirical direct connection between producing outputs and the ultimate outcome.

In many cases multiple outputs are required to accomplish an outcome. For example, a desired outcome of a public works or transportation department is improved road conditions. Road conditions are very poor when numerous potholes exist. One output of these entities is filling potholes. But if money were spent solely on filling potholes, imagine the kind of road that would result. (You may have actually experienced such a road.) Money must also be spent on repaving roads. Repaving roads is another output that contributes to the overall goal of improved road conditions.

IPOLO MODEL OF PERFORMANCE MEASURES

The IPOLO model can also be used to organize performance measures. Measures are simply numbers, so each component—input, process, output, or outcome— can be associated with one or more measures, or numbers. These measures are collected, reported, and interpreted to evaluate how well the organization is operating and whether it is achieving its goals.

Measurement is the process of assigning numbers to something according to a defined set of rules.

—Steven Medlin, iKon Group, inc.
(personal communication, July 2007)

Inputs. The input component contains one primary measure—dollars. As we described earlier, inputs are resources expended to produce work. In most instances organizations measure resources as dollars actually spent. Staff salaries are the major expense for most government and nonprofit organizations. In some cases the number of full-time-equivalent (FTE) staff can be substituted for salaries as an input measure. Input is the first box in the IPOLO model because without resources, work cannot be produced. In a school the salaries of teachers, administrators, and other staff are the major inputs. In the military the salaries and the cost of equipment are the major inputs. In snow removal the major inputs are the salaries of the drivers and the cost of equipment.

Inputs are resources expended on such things as salaries or equipment.

Process. Once again, a process is a series of steps or activities on which resources are expended and that result in the delivery of a product or service. A variety of performance measures represent how efficiently the process works, how timely it is, and how many mistakes are made during it. Before we expound on process measures, we must first consider the result of any process—outputs.

A process is a series of work steps that result in the delivery of a product or service.

Outputs. An output is simply a unit of work or volume of work completed. Depending on the nature of the product or service, outputs may be counted every minute, hour, day, week, or month. The number of checks generated by the Social Security Administration (SSA) in one hour or one day is an example of an SSA output. Government organizations can have many outputs. A state department of human services might have such output categories as the number of children placed in protective custody and the number of benefit applications processed. The number of telephone calls answered is an output from a customer call center. The numbers of people riding buses, obtaining business licenses, reviewing case files, arresting criminals, inspecting construction sites, and making payments are all examples of outputs.

Outputs are units of work produced by expending resources and completing the process.

Figure 2.3 illustrates the flow of the performance measurement process. Governments spend money, or inputs, to complete a process that results in one or more outputs. Several performance measures based on the calculation of the relationship between inputs and outputs represent how well the process is performing. More specifically, productivity refers to the ratio of outputs to inputs. A productivity score can be normalized or converted into a percentage for easier comparison. The inverse of productivity is unit cost, or the ratio of inputs to outputs. Unit cost is the cost to produce one unit of work. Because unit cost and productivity are computed from inputs and outputs, we place them under the input and output boxes in Figure 2.3.

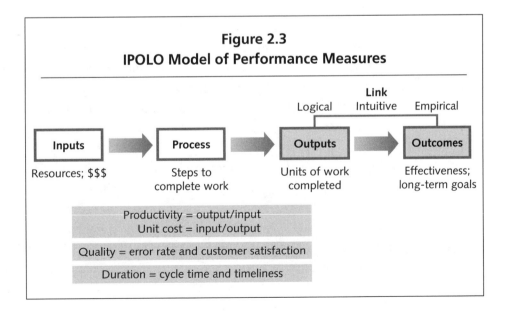

Figure 2.3
IPOLO Model of Performance Measures

Productivity is the ratio of outputs to inputs, or efficiency.

Unit cost is the ratio of inputs to outputs.

Another category of measures that falls under the process and output boxes relates to time. Cycle time is the actual time taken to complete a portion of the process or a certain number of process steps. Timeliness is the comparison of the cycle time to the performance standard and the interpretation of that comparison. Cycle time and timeliness fall under process and output because in many cases an organization is concerned about how long it takes for the process to result in a product. In some instances the length of time that a product is waiting for additional work is also measured.

Cycle time is the actual time taken to complete a process or process step.

For example, let's say you are applying for a business license. In brief, you complete the application on line, provide credit card payment information, and send the application to the city. The application is received by a processor, whose salary is considered input. The processor downloads and prints the application, reviews it for accuracy and completeness (quality measures), and sends it to a supervisor for approval. The supervisor approves the business license and mails it to you. From the time the processor receives your application to the time it is placed in the mail to you is the cycle time. The city has a goal of processing all business license applications within twenty-four hours. Because your license was mailed to you the same day your application was received, the city has been timely in its response. If the supervisor was on vacation for three days and your license was delayed as a result, the city would not be timely. If the city collected and reported performance measures, the report would include the amount of time the application sat waiting on the supervisor's desk. Table 2.1 offers more examples of performance measures.

One of the more confusing categories of measures is quality. We place quality under process and output because quality is usually associated with the characteristics of the output generated via the process. We encourage you to measure quality in one of two ways, both based on whether a product or service conforms to standards or expectations. In the first case the standards are characteristics that the product or service must possess. For example, a paycheck from your state

Table 2.1

Examples of Each Performance Measurement Category

PROCESS DESCRIPTION	INPUTS	OUTPUTS	OUTCOMES	QUALITY	CYCLE TIME
Treating patients in a hospital emergency room	Salary of physicians, nurses, receptionist; cost of equipment	Number of patients treated	Decreased mortality rates	Number of accurate diagnoses	Number of minutes waiting to be seen
Applying for a trade name	Salary of state employees that process applications	Number of trade name applications processed	Improved business relations	Number of errors in authorizing name	Number of hours or days to issue authorization
Conducting an audit	Salary of auditors	Number of audit findings	Improved performance and compliance of auditees	Number of recommendations accepted by the auditee	Number of months to complete and write the audit report
Registering students at a university	Salary of registration staff and cost of electronic processing	Number of students registered	Increase in online registration	Number of errors in billing or class registrations	Number of minutes to register for all classes

government employer is expected to have the correct name and amount. If it is written for a mistaken amount, that is considered an error. Quality can be measured by counting errors and comparing the number of errors to the total number of possible errors. This is called the *error rate*. A related measure is the number of complaints. A complaint is considered an error because it means the customer views the product or service as faulty.

Another way to measure quality is to compare performance to customer expectations. The performance improvement trends mentioned in Chapter One forever changed the government's perspective on the public. Most public organizations now view the public as customers of government products or services, and their satisfaction matters. This view has caused some debate. For example, can an arrested criminal be considered a customer? Yes. An accused car thief does not necessarily need to be satisfied with the overall outcome of the legal process. But he or she can and should have a reasonable expectation of receiving information in a timely manner and being treated with respect and dignity. Most government agencies now focus some resources on the public as customers, and many conduct surveys or focus groups. Surveys and focus groups must be administered and used carefully. When this is done, they can result in remarkable improvements in the way governments operate. For example, surveys of transit riders can lead to adjustments in schedules. Similarly, surveys of residents can lead to priority setting as a budget develops. Citizen surveys are becoming common and can be used as a measure of quality.

> *Quality is the error rate or the degree to which the outcome meets customer satisfaction.*

Outcomes. The last category is outcomes. Outcome measures are numbers associated with long-term strategies and goals. A logical, intuitive, or empirical link between outputs and outcomes should exist because the outcome is the ultimate reason that an organization spends the money on inputs, completes the process, and delivers the product or service. An appropriate number of high-quality, timely outputs should lead to a desired outcome. Commonly perceived links are sometimes tenuous and debatable. For example, if police arrest more criminals (number of arrests is the output), the community expects to see a decrease in the crime rate (outcome measure). However, one could argue that the crime rate is affected by many factors beyond the police department's control, such as high unemployment. Similarly, the IRS conducts individual audits (output is the number of audits completed) to help ensure overall compliance rates (outcome measure). However, the fear of personal tax audits and their possible results is only one factor that influences taxpayers' compliance with tax codes.

Outcomes are long-term consequences of the process and outputs.

Worksheet 2.1 will help you learn the terms discussed in this chapter. Worksheet 2.2 will help guide you through the process of developing measures for the process you are benchmarking. And Worksheet 2.3 will guide you through selecting appropriate measures for the benchmarking study itself. All worksheets are in the Resources in the back of the book.

PERFORMANCE MEASURES AND GOVERNMENT

In the 1980s, the U.S. General Accounting Office (recently renamed the Government Accountability Office [GAO]) conducted a series of management reviews of the Internal Revenue Service, the Social Security Administration, and several other government agencies. These management reviews included an evaluation of each agency's productivity, efficiency, and effectiveness. The reports revealed where high- and low-performing suborganizations were located in the agencies' offices throughout the United States. Recommendations were targeted at helping the low-performing offices in order to increase the average performance of all offices. At the time very little effort in government agencies was devoted to evaluating processes, managing costs, getting feedback from the public, or systematically improving performance.

The GAO studies indicate that by the 1980s, the federal government was already collecting and monitoring many different types of measures. In some cases the measures were regularly reported to managers, who in some instances acted on the measures by reassigning work. The IRS and SSA had spent millions of dollars on automated systems that reported performance measures, but they used these reports primarily to determine staffing patterns and project workloads. Although thousands of pages of performance measures were reported, relatively few were used beyond the budget and staffing processes. The GAO reports received very little attention from Congress. During that era Congress and the public were more interested in finding toilet seats and coffee pots that cost the military millions of dollars than in learning how government managers were using performance measures.

When total quality management and other performance improvement trends took hold in the United States, a wide variety of performance measures were in place, albeit used ineffectively or not at all. Performance improvement trends such as TQM, reinventing government, and the GPRA introduced ideas for more effective use of the measures that already existed and encouraged public employees to establish new or different measures when appropriate.

Improvement trends also introduced the idea that the public should be treated as customers of public sector products and services. Government agencies began to conduct focus groups and surveys to determine how well they performed in comparison with customers' expectations. In the twenty-first century most government and nonprofit organizations are using a wide array of performance measures to manage their resources and to demonstrate their performance to the public or their constituents. In fact the GPRA requires any organization that receives federal funds to establish performance measures and improvement initiatives. The GPRA also offers definitions of many performance measures and terms.

PERFORMANCE MEASURES AND MANAGEMENT

The trick to using performance measures to help you steer and manage well is to avoid being overwhelmed by the measurement process. Alex Jensen, city manager of Layton City, Utah, provides examples of just such a management style.

Layton, a distant suburb of Salt Lake City, is recognized throughout the state of Utah as a well-managed organization. Jensen experiences the usual challenges of managing a city, dealing with such issues as development, open space, and crime rates. When queried whether he regularly receives reports that include performance measures, Jensen (personal communication, January 2007) paused a moment before responding, "No. I guess I don't." But when asked how he knows how well the city and his staff are performing, he had a very different answer. Jensen explained that he holds regular staff meetings to talk about how each department is performing. Staff report on performance using various measures, such as outputs, cycle time, and customer satisfaction, to identify high and mediocre performance. Jensen's performance measure style is well integrated into Layton's management processes. He and his staff regularly bring needed resources or attention to areas of low performance.

Jensen's view is that performance measures should be used to identify performance problems to ensure that those problems are solved. He encourages a team approach and rarely if ever disciplines his staff in response to a performance measure. In Layton City, Jensen's informal measurement process fosters improvement while not overwhelming day-to-day activities.

IMPORTANCE OF MEASURES, COMPARISONS, AND BENCHMARKING

As stated earlier, benchmarking is a tool to improve performance. Measures, performance, and benchmarking are inextricably linked. An activity must be quantified or measured to determine, first, whether it is problematic and, second, whether the implementation of best practices or other actions have in fact improved it. Performance measures are compared in the benchmarking process.

Measures are important for many reasons. First, measures place performance in context by providing comparisons. The U.S. General Services Administration (GSA) established a goal to resolve 62 percent of supply discrepancies within thirty days. Staff reached this goal 71 percent of the time. On the surface this goal appeared to be reasonable and the level of performance quite good. When GSA staff benchmarked against a private sector firm, however, they discovered that their benchmarking partner had a goal of 100 percent resolution within one to three days and rarely failed to meet it. Once they discovered this private sector performance, GSA staff explored how the firm achieved it and ultimately imported several practices from this partner. Lesson number one, then, is that measures are important because they can change the way people view performance.

Second, measures reveal where organizations need to improve. The No Child Left Behind Act requires all schools to report test scores. Despite the controversy over this Act's assumptions and provisions, these scores illustrate to school administrators how well teachers are educating students and which subjects need more attention. Similarly, a city that calculates the actual cost of processing a business license can assess a fee based on that cost. When no cost information is available, the city does not know whether it is charging too little, enough, or too much.

Finally, managers need performance measures in the government and nonprofit sectors for managing on a daily, weekly, monthly, and even yearly basis. A single data point or measure tells managers very little. If government and nonprofit organizations are to operate efficiently and effectively, the leaders and managers of those organizations must have an ongoing gauge or dashboard to guide them.

In short, performance measures are important to benchmarking because they

- Allow comparisons among performances.
- Change the way performance is viewed.
- Reveal where improvements are needed.
- Demonstrate successful implementation of best practices.

Measures are vital to any benchmarking study. Measures can indicate to staff that performance needs improving. They can also demonstrate that an organization believed to be high performing is so in fact. It is not necessary to have identical measures in the benchmarking and partner organizations. However, when searching for promising practices to improve performance, the search must be grounded in numbers. An old auditor's saying applies here: "In God we trust—all others must have data."

SELECTING MEASURES FOR BENCHMARKING

Which are the optimum measures for use in benchmarking? It depends. We recommend that more than one measure be selected to represent each component in the IPOLO model. Here are a few things to keep in mind.

When benchmarking, the inputs must be resources that have been expended, not merely budgeted. If FTEs are used as a substitute, the actual number of FTEs should be used, not the budgeted number. Benchmarking examines what has happened in the past, not what is anticipated in the future. When conducting a benchmarking study, it is not necessary to struggle to define every penny of inputs, however. If the team is able to include 60 to 80 percent of the total inputs, and in most cases these inputs are salaries only, the study can proceed. The amount of time expended to gather all input costs can be quite high, and the added benefit of doing so quite low.

The process and output measures are closely linked. Outcomes result from efficient, high-quality, timely outputs, yet many intervening factors and externalities can disrupt the relationship between outputs and outcomes. Public and nonprofit sector staff, managers, and leaders have greater control over the inputs, process, and outputs than they do over the outcomes. Numerous methods exist to evaluate program outcomes, so focus benchmarking efforts on input, process, or output measures in the IPOLO performance measures model (Figure 2.3).

The performance measures an organization selects for tracking will be determined largely by the characteristics of the product or service delivered. For example, if you were looking to examine how well a 911 service was working, you would probably measure response time to emergency calls—not unit cost. A state department of transportation or a city or county department of public works should be interested in benchmarking various unit costs. Social service agencies might consider benchmarking the cycle time to process an application as well as the error rate in doing so. Virtually all public and nonprofit organizations can identify a partner for benchmarking customer satisfaction.

When selecting measures for your benchmarking study, ask the following questions:

❑ How does the measure illustrate the process or problem?

❑ Does the measure accurately and appropriately illustrate the process or problem?

❑ What types of measures are available?

❑ Are additional measures needed to conduct a benchmarking study?

❑ How reliable are the data collection systems for the measures?

❑ What measures are used by potential partners?

❑ What is the first reliable date on which the measure was collected and reported?

❑ Has the process or problem been represented by more than a single measure?

❑ Who has access to the measures?

❑ Will reports on the measures be readily available?

Answering these few basic questions about the measures will help the traditional benchmarking team determine how much time and energy will be required to collect and analyze data.

MEASUREMENT CHALLENGES IN THE PUBLIC AND NONPROFIT SECTORS

No public or nonprofit organization should be without a reliable collection of performance measures for decision making and day-to-day management.

Some unique aspects of public and nonprofit sectors create challenges in the measurement process. Although numbers are concrete and easy to understand, the data collection, the measurement process, and the results of measurement are imperfect and subject to interpretation. The imperfections are due partially to the nature of government. No private sector company is tasked with keeping the United States safe through military action or providing income security for the aged population. Safety and income security are difficult concepts to measure. Not impossible, just difficult.

Similarly, nonprofit organizations often fill gaps that result when government or private sector organizations do not fully meet people's service needs. For example, many nonprofit professional associations have been formed, such as the National League of Cities, Association of Government Accountants, Association for Women in Science, and the National Association of State Auditors, Comptrollers and Treasurers. Taxpayers are not likely to fund such organizations, because the taxpayer does not directly benefit from them. A private sector market does not exist, because members want and expect more than just an economic transaction between themselves and the association.

The nonprofit sector faces the additional challenge of measuring the productivity of volunteers. Salaries make up the primary input measure for the productivity equation. Volunteers are not paid, however, even though they make a significant contribution to the process and outputs. Thus nonprofit organizations do not have a clear picture of all inputs. Moreover, nonprofits are in the precarious position of losing volunteers if their performance or contribution is not acceptable or is misdirected. Rarely does a nonprofit terminate a relationship with a volunteer due to poor performance.

SUMMARY

- A measure is a quantity or number. Performance measures are a vital component of any benchmarking study.

- Benchmarking and measures provide information about relative performance.

- Performance measures are numbers that fall into the categories of input, output, process, or outcome.

- Most measures can be used in benchmarking projects, with the exception of outcome measures.

- Measures help governments and public sector organizations understand where to improve, when improvement is accomplished, and how to better direct programs and operations for increased efficiency and effectiveness.

PART TWO

Benchmarking Methods

I n this section we provide important information that will help you evaluate your organization's readiness for benchmarking and make two critical decisions before your study begins.

Chapter Three, "Preparing for Benchmarking," describes how a readiness assessment helps you determine whether your organization is truly prepared to conduct a benchmarking project. Asking a few basic questions can be quite revealing. In some cases organizations find that a benchmarking project should not proceed.

In addition, anyone interested in finding best practices must decide which of the two benchmarking methodologies is more appropriate to apply to the problem or process. This is the second critical decision, and the method selected will be determined partly by the scope of the problem or process. With these two decisions made, you will be ready to move ahead.

In this section we also describe the two benchmarking methodologies in detail. Think of Chapter Four, "The Traditional Benchmarking Method," and Chapter Five, "The Solution-Driven Benchmarking Method," as road maps designed to lead you to promising practices. These chapters provide ample instructions and examples from which both the novice and the experienced benchmarker will benefit.

Keep in mind that benchmarking is a tool and therefore does not always work if misused. Take time to understand the fundamental decisions before launching into a project.

Preparing for Benchmarking

During a training course delivered to Guam Memorial Hospital Authority (GMHA) staff, participants were asked to complete a benchmarking study of their respective organizations within the hospital. Some participants quickly moved ahead to benchmarking, but others did not. What was the difference? Readiness.

Although benchmarking and the search for best practices has become a widespread phenomenon, not all individuals or organizations are ready to benchmark. Many circumstances can prevent the successful launch of a benchmarking project. To ensure that you and your organization are fully prepared, take a few moments to complete two steps. First, answer a series of questions about readiness that will help to focus your project. Next, study and compare the two benchmarking methodologies, then select the one that is most appropriate for your process or problem. Investing a bit of time in these two steps will set the stage for you to maximize the benefits from whichever benchmarking method you select.

DETERMINE READINESS FOR BENCHMARKING

If you and your organization are really prepared for benchmarking, the answers to the following readiness questions will come quickly. Spending a moment to review these questions should build your confidence and reconfirm your selection of the process or problem to be benchmarked. If you stumble on a question or two or find yourself unsure about the answer, it would be wise to think about the issues raised by the question. Slow down and take a little time to ponder the implications. An ounce of prevention is worth a pound of cure.

Readiness Questions

1. What evidence suggests we are ready to benchmark?
2. Is the initiative related to strategic issues?
3. Will our customers or constituents benefit from the results?
4. What characterizes the process or problem?
5. Are we prepared to devote the necessary resources to the project?

What Evidence Suggests You Are Ready to Benchmark?

Some of the GMHA staff mentioned earlier had clear evidence that they were ready to benchmark but others did not. Participants from the food services and housekeeping divisions had a good understanding of their respective processes. They were able to illustrate their processes through flowcharts or lists of steps. Each of these divisions had developed performance measures that were used to evaluate their area. Each was ready for the next step—benchmarking to improve performance.

Conversely, the participants from the facilities division were struggling to define the work-order process and to obtain basic performance measures because these measures were collected in four different computer systems. Similarly, the pharmacy had never counted the number of prescriptions issued on each day, week, or month. Output measures were difficult to compile. Both functions lacked fundamental information to clearly identify or define a performance problem. Benchmarking is about improving performance. When current performance is unknown, a benchmarking project can be a waste of time and resources.

You are prepared to benchmark a process when you have evidence that allows you to

❏ Demonstrate a good understanding of how the process works.

❏ Establish a baseline performance through performance measures.

❏ Be confident (perhaps on the basis of e-mails or memos) that staff are receptive to new ways of completing the work.

I was surprised, but GMHA was definitely ready to benchmark. Leaders and managers were anxious to learn what others had done to improve performance.

—Steven Medlin, iKon Group, inc.
(personal communication, July 2007)

Is the Initiative Related to Strategic Issues?

During the course of its normal operations, an organization identifies core products and services—that is, activities critical to its success—and many areas ripe for performance improvement. Many of these processes, products, services, activities, and areas have strategic importance to the organization—that is, they are related to accomplishing the desired outcomes or strategic goals. For example, highway repair is a strategic issue for state departments of transportation because the repairs are essential to the effective execution of the department's strategic goal of maintaining safe roads. Food services in a hospital or school are related to the strategic goal of providing a healthy environment for patients and students. In contrast, cleaning roadside litter, selling pencils, or operating a gift shop is distant from the desired accomplishments of departments of transportation, school systems, and hospitals, respectively. Circumstances may exist that would encourage benchmarking these areas, but the impact on the desired outcome will be less than other benchmarking efforts produce. (Remember, outcome is the ultimate purpose of an organization.) You are ready to benchmark when improvements are expected to have a positive impact on strategic accomplishments.

Will Customers or Constituents Benefit from the Results?

External pressures are often the forces that create the momentum for benchmarking in public sector organizations, and they often influence the choice of what to benchmark. Public dissatisfaction or even outrage frequently prompts the search for best practices. For instance, a major East Coast city entered into a study of emergency medical services (EMS) after several citizens died waiting for EMS teams to arrive. The city and county had been at odds about who should respond within some areas with overlapping boundaries. Competitive pressure, so evident in the trend to privatize public sector activities, can also motivate agencies to seek out and import best practices. One of the criteria the Bertelsmann Foundation uses for its city management award is the demonstrated commitment of the city to its citizens and customers. This criterion assesses the extent to which the local government sees itself as a service provider that gears its services to the needs of its citizens. The impact on the citizens or constituents should be an important factor in deciding to benchmark.

What Characterizes the Process or Problem?

Essentially, this question asks whether you have weighed the costs associated with benchmarking against the benefits expected from importing best practices. To select an appropriate process or problem, ask the following questions:

- ❏ Has the process or problem created enough difficulties to warrant benchmarking?
- ❏ Is improvement possible?
- ❏ Is benchmarking the appropriate approach for improving the process or solving the problem?
- ❏ Is there a sufficient gap between existing performance and desired performance to warrant an investment in benchmarking?
- ❏ Has the process or problem caused uncomfortable relations with customers or the media?
- ❏ Are the people who work in the process ready for benchmarking?

If you can answer yes to most or all of these questions, you have probably selected a good process or problem for benchmarking, one where the benefits will outweigh the costs.

Are You Prepared to Devote the Necessary Resources to the Project?

As part of meeting the requirement of the Government Performance and Results Act and the U.S. Office of Management and Budget (OMB) that agencies demonstrate performance improvement, the U.S. Environmental Protection Agency

(EPA) completed the Program Assessment Review Tool (PART). One recommendation from the PART was that the EPA benchmark its processes as a way to improve performance. The Superfund billing process was selected as the subject of the benchmarking study, partly because of the wide variations among regional areas in billing for Superfund cleanups. Also, baseline performance had been established.

The EPA prepared for the benchmarking in two ways. First, senior officials made it clear to agency staff that the project was going to happen, and they communicated the reason for doing so. Second, senior officials installed a project manager, Melanie Hoff, to coordinate the efforts, and they funded training for project participants. By communicating to staff, designating a project manager, and allocating funds for training, EPA management clearly demonstrated that it was serious about supporting the entire benchmarking project.

Use Worksheet 3.1, in the Resources, to evaluate your own organization's readiness for benchmarking.

SELECT A BENCHMARKING METHOD

Compare the Steps

The steps in the traditional benchmarking method have not changed significantly over the past twenty-five years. Numerous books and consultants have promoted some variations on these steps, but even these variations share several basic characteristics. The traditional method we present in the next chapter consists of eleven steps. The first step is to assess the organization's readiness, as just described, and to charter a team to complete a benchmarking study. Once the readiness level is acceptable, a leader or manager in the organization taps a small group of people and tasks them with improving a process. The traditional method focuses on benchmarking a process because it is within a process that products and services (outputs) are developed. If a product or service is faulty, inappropriate, or not meeting expectations, the problem usually can be traced to steps in that development process.

The traditional benchmarking team spends much time defining and analyzing the process in question. Flowcharts are frequently used to illustrate steps in the process, and performance measures are collected and displayed in a way that makes process performance easy to see. The team carefully examines the process before selecting partners with whom to benchmark. Once benchmarking partners are identified, the team visits them to observe and compare processes and data. Team members identify best or promising practices and create an implementation strategy. The team then develops recommendations and reports for the leader or manager who chartered the team. Once approved, the best practice is adapted, imported, and monitored to ensure success. The traditional benchmarking method requires about six months to complete and may take as long as twelve months. (We present a detailed discussion of all the steps in the traditional benchmarking method in Chapter Four.)

The solution-driven benchmarking method is much less time consuming and begins in a very different way. An individual or small group discovers a problem that needs immediate attention. The problem is briefly analyzed, using measures or data that currently exist. Measures are also used to establish criteria for performance goals and for demonstrating improvement. The individual or group then searches for a solution; group members may work individually at this point. Personal and professional contacts are accessed, and the Internet is thoroughly searched. A list of possible best practices is developed, and these practices are evaluated for feasibility. The most promising practice is implemented, and a brief period of monitoring occurs. This solution-driven method can be completed in a few days or months. (Our detailed discussion of the steps in this method appears in Chapter Five.) See Table 3.1 for an outline of the steps in both methods.

Understand the Conceptual Differences

An analogy may help to illustrate the differences between the traditional and solution-driven methods. Imagine an old rotary dial telephone. You may remember how cumbersome it was to poke a finger into the hole over the number you wanted and rotate the dial to the hook, where you were forced to stop. The dial then slowly swung back to its original place, and you poked your finger into the hole over the second number. You repeated this process until all the numbers were dialed and you placed your call. It was difficult to misdial, partially because of the relationship between the holes and the numbers and because of the placement of the holes on an easy-to-maneuver dial. Then a breakthrough came with touch-tone dialing, which employed a keypad similar to a calculator's. No more waiting for the dial to swing back into place. Now there is speed dialing, allowing

Table 3.1
Steps in the Traditional and Solution-Driven Methods

TRADITIONAL BENCHMARKING	SOLUTION-DRIVEN BENCHMARKING
1. Charter a team.	1. Discover the problem.
2. Determine the purpose and scope of the benchmarking initiative.	2. Establish criteria for solutions.
	3. Search for promising practices.
3. Clearly define the process or function you intend to benchmark.	4. Implement promising practices.
	5. Monitor progress.
4. Research potential benchmarking partners.	
5. Choose performance measures.	
6. Collect internal data to establish baseline performance.	
7. Collect data from the partner organization.	
8. Analyze the performance gap between processes.	
9. Import practices in order to close the performance gap.	
10. Regularly monitor results after implementing changes.	
11. Reevaluate changes and start anew.	

users to place a call simply by pressing one button. Traditional benchmarking is not antiquated like rotary dial telephones, but it is similar in that it requires a certain patience and sequencing of events to successfully complete the task. Solution-driven benchmarking is quick and efficient although not quite as fast as speed dialing. The leap from dial telephones to touch-tone calling was significantly aided by technology, as was the jump from traditional to solution-driven benchmarking. And regardless of the level of technology, people end up with the same result—they reach the desired person or the best practice.

Another analogy might also help. If you imagine that the search for promising or best practices is a search for gold, you can think about the traditional approach as similar to a treasure hunt. Imagine a group of pirates poring over a treasure map with a big X that marks the spot where the gold is buried. The pirates work together to sail to the right island, paddle to land, find their way through the trees, ford alligator-infested streams, locate the spot, dig up the gold, and carry it home. A treasure hunt is very systematic. One misjudgment or step in the wrong direction may cause the pirates to miss the gold. Similarly, the traditional approach requires that a team focus on completing the required steps in the right order. If steps are skipped or condensed, the team may be unable to dig up the best practice.

The solution-driven approach looks much more like the California gold rush and the forty-niners. Most of the forty-niners worked as individuals, believing they could find their fortune simply by looking in the right place. While purchasing supplies in the San Francisco area, they frequently talked to other gold miners about potential locations, hazards, and advice for finding the gold. The forty-niners worked independently yet seemed to rely on a network of information to help them choose the right supplies, location, defenses, and potential for wealth. When gold was found, others rushed to search in the surrounding areas. Similarly, the solution-driven method is usually taken up by someone who believes that a problem needs to be solved. The individual (in some cases two or three individuals) looks for organizations or situations where energy has already been devoted to the problem. Where has the gold surfaced in the past? What have others already discovered? The individual essentially pans the available resources for the best practices.

The process of the pirates conducting a treasure hunt is more complicated and detailed than the process of the forty-niners seeking fortunes during the gold rush. The gold rush approach is charged with energy and depends more on an individual's ability to tap surrounding resources than on a team's ability to interpret a map and surrounding landscape. Nonetheless both can yield rich results.

Compare the Characteristics

The traditional method and the solution-driven method can be compared and contrasted in other ways. Keep in mind that the following are generalities to improve your understanding of the differences and to ensure that you choose the best method for your benchmarking study. See Table 3.2 for an outline comparison of the following characteristics.

Table 3.2
Comparative Characteristics of the Traditional Method
and the Solution-Driven Method

CHARACTERISTIC	TRADITIONAL	SOLUTION-DRIVEN
Complexity of benchmarking process	Complex	Simple
Management involvement	High	Low to medium
Leader or executive involvement	Medium	Low to high
Resource requirements	High	Low
Process focus	High	Low
Problem focus	Low	High
Dependence on measures	High	Medium
Practicality for governments or NGOs	Large or complex organizations	Small to medium-sized organizations

Complexity. The traditional method requires eleven steps whereas the solution-driven method requires only five. The traditional method is more complex not only because of the larger number of steps but also because each of those eleven steps requires more time and energy to complete than each of the five steps does in the solution-driven method. The solution-driven method is streamlined and flexible.

Management involvement. The traditional method requires midlevel managers to be very involved in the benchmarking project. In many cases they participate on the benchmarking team and in site visits, determine priorities for implementation, and have primary responsibility for long-term success. Midlevel managers are not necessarily involved in the solution-driven method unless they are the ones conducting the study. If midlevel managers have staff completing solution-driven benchmarking, they may be peripherally involved in approving changes or implementing promising practices discovered by others.

Leader or executive involvement. In a traditional benchmarking study the organization's leaders or executives are somewhat involved at the beginning or end of the study. They approve the team's charter, receive periodic briefings, and approve final recommendations. They are much less involved in solution-driven benchmarking unless they are specifically asked to identify professional contacts or networks for promising practices.

Resource requirements. Organizations typically allow traditional benchmarking teams to spend most of their time on the project for about six months, making it very resource intensive. The team members may be drawn from different parts of the organization and are sometimes geographically dispersed. And implementation of best practices can be time consuming and can require the investment of additional staff or fiscal resources. The traditional method often includes a site visit to partner organizations, which requires financial resources for travel. Conversely, one individual using the solution-driven method may spend a few hours or days locating best practices. Implementation of promising practices can be quick and easy due to the smaller project scope and reduced need to analyze alternatives. The exception occurs when implementation of a promising practice requires cooperation or contributions from multiple units within the larger organization.

Process or problem focus. Traditional benchmarking usually focuses on a process that has been problematic. This method's underlying philosophy is that faulty processes lead to most of an organization's problems. If staff fix the process, their problem will be resolved. Solution-driven benchmarking recognizes that not all problems are caused by poor process performance. Its goal is to find the best solutions to problems, and it does not require process analysis. In some cases solution-driven benchmarking is used when no process currently exists and instead a process, operation, or policy must be installed.

Dependence on measures. Measures play an important role in both methods but more so in traditional benchmarking. Measures are used to clearly define and illustrate poor process performance. Solution-driven benchmarking uses measures primarily to define criteria for success. Less time is spent on analyzing measures related to the problem.

Practicality for governments and NGOs. Although both benchmarking methods can be used by large and small government and public sector organizations, a large organization will have more resources to devote to a traditional benchmarking study. Also, a large organization may have suborganizations in different locations, and this dispersion may create opportunities to compare and find best practices without looking externally. By large organization, we mean one with over 250 staff members or a budget over $1 million. Small organizations may have greater success with the solution-driven approach because it is less resource intensive. Also, smaller organizations may have fewer obstacles to overcome while implementing the best practices. A smaller staff, fewer policies, and greater flexibility facilitate solution-driven benchmarking.

More Selection Guidance

If you have a reasonable understanding of the differences between the traditional and solution-driven benchmarking methods described in this chapter, selecting the right one should be quite easy. But some additional guidance may still be helpful. Select the traditional benchmarking method when you can agree with the following statements:

- ❑ The problem or process crosses several organizational boundaries.
- ❑ A variety of individuals must be involved in solving the problem or streamlining the process.
- ❑ Extensive data analysis is required.
- ❑ The solution is not supposed to solve an urgent problem or immediate crisis.
- ❑ Performance over time is inconsistent or poor, regardless of prior efforts to improve.
- ❑ A team can be formed and its members can dedicate a sufficient amount of time to complete the project.
- ❑ The organization's culture may need to be changed.
- ❑ Various individuals or groups must buy into the solution.
- ❑ Significant organizational changes are not already underway.

Select the solution-driven benchmarking method when you can agree with the following statements:

- ❑ Time is of the essence.
- ❑ Resources are limited.
- ❑ Implementation of a promising practice is not likely to require a change in the organization's culture.

❏ The problem does not cross a large number of organizational boundaries.

❏ The leader, manager, or supervisor does not need a lot of buy-in from others to implement the best practice.

Chapters Four and Five describe the methods in detail and provide case examples. Few, if any, of the cases precisely follow the benchmarking steps, and we consider this a good thing. Regardless of the method, each organization and benchmarking study is unique. We encourage you to seriously consider the intent and importance of each step and adapt it to your unique situation. Similarly, best or promising practices discovered while benchmarking should be closely scrutinized and adjusted to suit the unique needs of the importing organization.

The checklist in Worksheet 3.2, in the Resources, will help you select the correct benchmarking method for your organization.

MAJOR BENCHMARKING PITFALLS

Benchmarking organizations make three major mistakes that are the most frequent causes of project difficulties or even failure:

1. *The organization assumes that a search for best practices means looking for the best practices in the broad external world and then importing them.* This naïveté is a sign of low organizational readiness. Research and experience suggest that benchmarking with widely dissimilar organizations or with organizations that have very different processes may actually harm any quality improvement implementation. Practitioners who honestly, thoroughly, and openly appraise their agency's readiness level and select processes for benchmarking that are appropriate for that level avoid the difficulties of being in over their heads.

2. *The scope of the practice selected is wrong.* Many improvement efforts fail because the topic selected is too broad (for example, "simplify taxes"), too narrow ("simplify item 14 on the tax form"), or unclear ("make it easier to comply with the tax code"). Benchmarking initiatives run into similar problems when the scope of the effort is unclear, too broad, or too narrow. Scrutinizing the selection process to clarify your scope will help your organization avoid making this mistake.

3. *The organization tries to tackle too many processes at once, so the benchmarking process is not focused.* Remember that benchmarking is not the solution for all

organizational performance problems nor can it be applied to all the organizational problems for which it is the best approach. An organization needs to focus its benchmarking activities on the critical, strategic processes that most affect the quality and cost of public services. For example, when West Virginia's employee-training benchmarking team began to consider what aspect of training to focus on, the oversight team gave the benchmarking team a helpful statement of goals: "To ensure that state employees receive the training they need to deliver quality services to taxpayers; to instill value in training; and to establish a formal 'corporate university' to ensure high quality and consistency in program development, instruction, and administration." The scope of the project was refined after the consultant recommended that the team narrow its focus to process rather than content. The team's mandate became to devise an effective employee-training delivery system.

An organization that thoughtfully selects a process to benchmark can avoid these common mistakes. Thoughtfully selecting a process is one of the most difficult parts of benchmarking. Once it is completed your organization is ready to begin the exciting, energizing, and educational phase of the effort. Over the next few months, you will clearly define the process, measure its performance, select benchmarking partners, and come to understand their processes. As with any journey, the route you select determines what you experience and learn, the length and expense of your trip, the obstacles or detours that you encounter, and ultimately, whether you reach your destination.

Chapters Four and Five offer two maps for that journey—how to use the traditional benchmarking method and how to use the solution-driven approach. Either one can lead to promising practices and performance improvement.

SUMMARY

- Individuals and organizations can answer a series of questions to ensure they are ready to complete a benchmarking study.

- The traditional benchmarking method uses about eleven steps to find best practices whereas the solution-driven method requires about five steps.

- Both benchmarking methods use performance measures to reveal where problems exist, when performance improves, and when problems have been resolved.

- Select the traditional approach when ample resources and time are available and when the problem or process crosses several organizational boundaries.

- Select the solution-driven approach when less time or fewer resources are available.

- For the best results adapt your chosen method's steps to your organization's circumstances.

The Traditional Benchmarking Method

The traditional benchmarking method encourages continuous improvement through the discovery of best practices, but it has additional benefits. Traditional benchmarking forces an organization to ask why it is operating in the current manner. "Why are we providing these services?" "Why are we conducting business this way?" "Why haven't we solved this problem before?" Often the questions of why are lost in the day-to-day shuffle of operating an organization. Traditional benchmarking requires an organization to slow down, take a step back, and reevaluate its goals and mission.

Benchmarking also requires organizations to identify ways to measure their services in terms of inputs and outcomes. In today's information age, organizations seem to collect data on everything. Sometimes they are not the right data, however, and organizational inefficiencies are allowed to spiral into worse performance. Traditional benchmarking requires organizations to identify measures important to their operations and to systematically evaluate these measures.

Traditional benchmarking also reduces the need for organizations to reinvent the wheel. The search for organizational solutions may require a series of trial-and-error projects that could be costly, time-consuming, and ultimately detrimental. However, implementing best practices that have proven successful for other organizations may reduce the cost of finding an appropriate solution. As organizations become better at benchmarking, the benefits of benchmarking accrue at a faster rate. Once an organization completes its first successful benchmarking study it will be easier to do the second time and perhaps will be done with greater success.

OTHER VIEWS OF THE BENCHMARKING METHODS

As discussed in Chapter One, the corporate method of benchmarking significantly influenced the public sector to explore the methodology. The corporate style is a traditional approach that is narrow and analytical. The formal steps must be pursued in a sequential order. However, not everyone agrees on which steps must be executed, the order of these steps, or the total number of steps. We found examples of traditional benchmarking ranging from four to eleven or twelve steps. Those with fewer steps rarely skip formal steps, however; rather they collapse or combine pieces of the process.

Dozens of benchmarking models are offered to the public and private sectors. The recent *Department of the Navy Benchmarking Handbook* (Kraft, 1997) reviews some of these models, including AT&T's twelve-step process; Michael Spendolini's eleven steps; Texas Instrument's and Xerox's ten steps; GTE's five steps; and the U.S. Air Force's four-step model. A review of the traditional benchmarking steps offered by scholars, practitioners, and organizations could continue for pages and pages. However, the point is simple. The formal or traditional benchmarking steps may vary slightly but remain largely the same throughout all the approaches.

The eleven-step methodology offered in our first edition remains essentially unchanged in this edition. This method accomplishes two goals by using more steps than most other methods. First, it keeps the benchmarking team on track through simple, sequential actions. Second, team members are not required to work to give greater definition to broadly defined steps.

ELEVEN-STEP TRADITIONAL BENCHMARKING METHOD

Consider the following steps a road map to promising practices. Use common-sense judgment in deciding where more or less time should be spent along the way. Don't rush to the next step. (Figure 4.1 summarizes the method.)

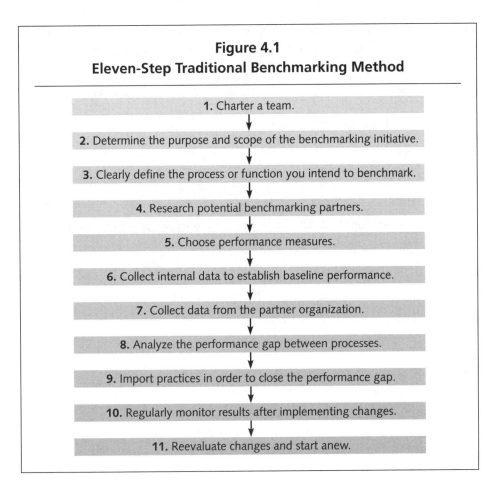

Figure 4.1
Eleven-Step Traditional Benchmarking Method

1. Charter a team.

2. Determine the purpose and scope of the benchmarking initiative.

3. Clearly define the process or function you intend to benchmark.

4. Research potential benchmarking partners.

5. Choose performance measures.

6. Collect internal data to establish baseline performance.

7. Collect data from the partner organization.

8. Analyze the performance gap between processes.

9. Import practices in order to close the performance gap.

10. Regularly monitor results after implementing changes.

11. Reevaluate changes and start anew.

1. Charter a Team

A traditional benchmarking study cannot be completed unless a team is created to carry it out. Ideally, team members are drawn from various parts of the organization and possess expertise or experience in areas related to the benchmarking subject. The teams we discuss later formed by the Environmental Protection Agency (EPA) and the Department of the Interior's Mineral Management Service (MMS) each had five members. A three-person team may be too small, but an eight- to ten-person team may be too large. Also consider that teams with an odd number of members will never face a tie vote when making decisions.

Teams have several important activities to complete before they begin a benchmarking study. At a minimum they need to review the readiness questions listed in Chapter Three and select the appropriate benchmarking method. Additionally, teams should meet with the individual or the leadership group that chartered them. Here are a few questions for team members to ask:

- What expectations do you have for a final product?
- Why was this benchmarking team chartered?
- Why were these members selected to participate?
- Are you the primary audience for our recommendations?
- What assurances can you give that the recommendations will be implemented?
- What resources (financial and staff) are available to support the team?
- Whom should we contact when we encounter red tape, obstacles, uncooperative staff, or other problems?
- Will you provide training on the benchmarking process?
- Will you ensure that we have timely access to data?

The team executes the benchmarking study on behalf of the chartering individual or group. The team depends on the authority held by that individual or group to ensure resources are available and other staff in the organization cooperate with the team.

2. Determine Purpose and Scope of Project

Deciding what to benchmark does not define the purpose of the project. An agency may benchmark a single process for many different reasons, hoping to achieve many different results. Suppose a state decided to benchmark its driver's license application process. The purpose of the project could be to decrease cycle time, increase customer satisfaction, decrease process cost, or reduce the number of traffic accidents or the number of driving-under-the-influence infractions. Some reasons for benchmarking may actually conflict with expected results. For example, reducing cycle time might cause higher costs if it requires more staff or better equipment. It is critical to the success of the benchmarking project that all those involved debate its purpose (the reasons for doing it and the expectations for it) and agree on and document that purpose before the project gets started.

The scope of a project must be written down and must delineate clear boundaries for exactly what the project should study. There may also be time, resource, or other limits placed on the project, but certain key questions have to be answered—for example, where does the process being benchmarked begin? Where does it end? What are the limits of this process that separate it from other processes?

A clearly defined scope that is carefully controlled throughout the project is essential to successful benchmarking. Scopes that are too broad or too narrow or that suffer *scope creep* cause many benchmarking efforts to founder. In the driver's license application process, does the process begin when the state mails out the application? When the citizen receives the notice? When the citizen sends in an application? When the state receives the application? The answer to this relatively simple question, "Where does the process begin?" will have a dramatic effect on the results expected, the partners chosen for benchmarking, and the kinds of best practices that are found. Similar issues—concerning, for example, where the process ends, its relationships to other processes, how much time the project has, and whether legislative changes are acceptable—must be addressed if the project is to proceed efficiently.

Scope creep is the scourge of many benchmarking projects. A project usually starts with a clear, tightly defined scope. But as the work gets under way, members of the project team, stakeholders, benchmarking partners, and numerous other interested parties often find other processes they want the benchmarking team to look at. Soon the scope has become unwieldy, the focus of the project has been lost, and the additional burden placed on the project brings it to its knees.

Changes to the project purpose or scope need to be managed just as closely as the benchmarking effort itself. Proposed changes should go through the same type of scrutiny, discussion, and decision making used to develop selection criteria for potential benchmarking topics, to identify a process for benchmarking, and to come to agreement on the need to conduct a benchmarking study in the first place. If a good readiness assessment was completed as described in Chapter Three, any benchmarking team will breeze through this step. Conversely, teams place themselves at great risk of failure if the parameters listed here are not clear.

3. Clearly Define the Process or Function You Intend to Benchmark

Analyze your internal processes to get a thorough understanding of what is really going on. Dig under the surface of the process to grasp the true driving forces behind each performance measure. Create high-level flowcharts, and verify their accuracy with people who contribute to the process. Consider talking with process customers or stakeholders to get an idea of how they would see performance improvements. Add permanent or temporary team members if these additional members will increase the level of understanding about the process.

4. Research Potential Partners

This tends to be the step that benchmarking teams most enjoy. Researching potential partners is energizing, informative, and simple, especially compared to ten years ago. The Internet may be the best source for identifying potential partners. Be sure to search the Web pages of professional associations and award programs. Don't forget to consider a private sector partner for your government or nonprofit organization. A first step is to establish criteria for selecting a partner. Consider these partner characteristics:

- Organization type, as compared to your own
- Geographic location
- Demographics
- Technology
- Demonstrated performance
- Receipt of awards or recognition for performance

Once you identify a few potential partners, inquire of each one whether its staff would consider sharing information for your benchmarking study. Be sure you are prepared to explain the purpose, scope, timeline, and other details of your project, as well as the reason you are interested in partnering with this other organization. If you identify several potential partners and talk with all of them, one will likely surface as having the greatest potential to help. Select one of the partners, let the others know your decision, and move ahead to the next step. One partner is likely to yield enough ideas and promising practices for one benchmarking team to handle. Also, be careful not to make commitments that you cannot keep. In your excitement to develop the partnership, be sure you do not commit to a site visit unless you are certain of the timeframe, funding, and your team's ability to conduct this visit. Similarly, do not commit to give the partner something in return, such as data or the final report, if the information is sensitive.

5. Choose Performance Measurements

Numerous participants in our benchmarking training classes were surprised that the step of choosing performance measures did not occur until after selecting a partner. Their argument was that a benchmarking team needs performance measures before this to find partners and that presumably the process selected for benchmarking was chosen because performance measures demonstrated that it was performing poorly. They would assert that the sequence we displayed must be a mistake.

These are valid questions and concerns. We reiterate that the sequence of steps is less important than actually completing each step. If a team has settled on performance measures prior to selecting a partner, the project will not fall apart. However, two good reasons exist for not forcing the issue until this step. First, if the members of the benchmarking team are wedded to certain measures, they may not consider partners who do not have those particular measures. In doing so they may overlook some promising practices. For example, a team benchmarking fire prevention may eliminate some potential partners because of large dollar losses in property in the service area. The benchmarking team has focused on dollars lost as a key measure of performance and assumes lower is better. However, a fire district may have potential as a partner because it was recognized and awarded for efforts with smoke detectors and school programs, and the large loss may be attributable to arson or an industrial problem. Similarly, if a team that is benchmarking emergency response limits itself to looking at length of time from call to arrival, it may overlook best practices at the dispatch or site level. What is the number of rings before calls are answered? What life-saving equipment is available to the ambulance crew? Getting to the scene quickly may not be the only factor in high-performing emergency response.

Second, the measures may become the overriding issue instead of only a part of the study. One city's benchmarking team insisted that the number of customer complaints received by the mayor was the most important measure to benchmark. Team members believed most people didn't call the various city departments because constituents rarely understand how their local government is organized. The team members wrestled for several meetings with how to collect and analyze data about the nature of the call, the location of the constituent, and the referral to the department resolving the problem. When selecting partners, the team almost overlooked potential partners who had centralized their constituent services, including complaints to the mayor or city manager, into a call center (these were large cities). The high-performing cities had plenty of other data and many best practices to share related to constituent complaints. What's the bottom line? Be flexible on performance measures until you find partners. Then decide which measures are most important. Also take care to choose a set of measures that is comprehensive yet commonly used for the chosen process or function. Refer to Chapter Two for additional information.

6. Collect Internal Data to Establish Baseline Performance

Governments and nonprofits do not appear to lack measures; they simply do not always use them. Some measures probably exist for most processes selected for benchmarking. If so, this step asks the team to collect and analyze these data in a way that illustrates performance over time. In some cases the benchmarking team will need to request that a special report be generated with the information. The Guam Memorial Hospital Authority teams had to request several special staff reports before they could analyze outputs relative to inputs. Fortunately, one of the management information system (MIS) staff was a benchmarking team member and could see to it that the reports were timely and generated accurately. Requests for special data runs can delay the project and teams can encounter red tape. Special requests to the MIS department must be integrated into day-to-day computer operations and cannot always be completed immediately. A benchmarking team making such requests should be prepared to wait a reasonable amount of time before pounding the MIS staff for results.

The period of time covered by the data will vary, depending on how frequently outputs are delivered. Use six to twelve months as a guide. In most instances the process performance can be illustrated through a minimum of six months of data. Once about twenty-four months of data have been analyzed, analysis of additional data will be less meaningful, although not without some benefit. Be sure the data collection process has been consistent over the time period. Also, when using multiple measures, use identical time periods for data collection for all measures.

7. Collect Data from Partner Organizations

By now someone from the benchmarking team has made an exploratory call to the potential partner. A partner should be expecting this step but cannot respond until the request is made. This call should be courteous and take as little time and be as little bother as possible, but do not sacrifice data reliability to these needs. Be specific about the information or measures you are requesting. Provide the time frame, type of data, and other relevant information. Be sure the time period over which you collect the internal data matches the time period for the data collected from the partner. Request the data from the partner before any site visits are planned.

This is another step in the benchmarking process that can become more efficient through use of technology. For example, the Utah Benchmarking Project (which we discuss in Chapter Six) created a survey instrument that was distributed on line for participating cities to respond to. Use of the Internet and Web-based communication can reduce the time needed for and cost of collecting data from partner organizations.

8. Analyze the Performance Gap Between Processes

Gap analysis identifies the differences between your process and that of your benchmarking partner. The gap may be a performance difference, reflected in the performance measures, or it may be a process difference, indicated by differences in how the process operates. The goal of the gap analysis is not for the benchmarking team to identify differences between its process and its partner's process but for the team to understand why there are differences. What is it about one process that makes it better than another? What practices produce better performance? What are the drivers of the performance measures? The search for answers to these questions leads to the identification of best practices. By determining the factors that make one process operate better than another, the team also finds the information it needs to change those factors in its own organization.

9. Import Practices in Order to Close Gap

Once the benchmarking team has identified a practice or practices that can improve the performance of its process, its organization prepares to import the best practice. Rarely is the practice introduced exactly as it is carried out in the partner organization. The practice must be adapted to the importing organization. There is no need to wait until the entire benchmarking study is completed before introducing a new practice. If the team finds a best practice that can be imported immediately and will improve the process right away, it can go ahead and use it.

The gap analysis completed in the previous step identifies where the benchmarking team's organization can improve and also some of the changes required to bring about this improvement. This information needs to be translated into specific actions, milestones, and responsible individuals if it is to be successfully used to improve performance, however. Thus the benchmarking team needs to develop an action plan for implementing the best practices that clearly states the action to be taken, when it needs to be done, and who is to do it.

One of the great obstacles to organizational change is the inevitable resistance of those being asked to make the change. They cannot be allowed to prevent the introduction of the new process. If a best practice is to be implemented successfully, the managers, employees, stakeholders, and other interested parties must be included in the decision and implementation process. Sharing the data from the benchmarking study, the gap analysis, the best practice, and the plans for importing the practice with all of these constituencies will elicit their support and involvement, which are essential to the success of the new best practice. The managers and employees who are using the current process are often especially helpful in figuring out how to import the best practice.

Even an exceptionally good benchmarking study will be a failure if the best practice is not imported successfully. Organizations are typically very good at conducting studies but weak at the hard work and follow-through needed to make the recommendations from those studies take root in organizational operations.

10. Regularly Monitor Results After Implementing Changes

A recently imported best practice requires special care, attention, and nurturing. Otherwise it runs the risk of fading away or reverting to the previous process from lack of support and follow-through. The benchmarking sponsor, team members, and stakeholders need to be especially vigilant during the implementation and early operation of the new practice to ensure that it is installed in a way that is faithful to its design (that is, that it is implemented and operated as the benchmarking study recommended) and that it is producing the intended results.

When the best practice is implemented fully in the organization, both the way in which it is implemented and the results it is achieving should be followed carefully. The best practice needs to be installed in the way that was intended, as just described, and the factors affecting the success of the new process need to be watched and adjusted as needed. Are the operators of the process sufficiently trained? Do the owners of the process receive accurate, timely feedback on its operation? How are the processes that provide inputs to and take outputs from the new process handling the new way of doing work? What are the performance measures for the new process? Is it achieving what was intended?

The ultimate measure of the success of a best practice is whether the performance measures for the process improve. After all, the search for best practices is not an academic exercise; it is a means to an end—a way to improve organizational performance. If performance measures do not reflect improvement, you can get to the source of the problem in several ways. You can examine the process to see if the best practice was implemented properly or needs to be modified to provide its full benefit in the new setting; or you may need to study the processes and systems surrounding the new practice to see if they are having an adverse effect on the process. New processes sometimes take a while to reach full performance, so the performance measures can be tracked over time to determine if the process is improving.

In some cases the measurement system itself has to be reconsidered. The measures used for the old process may not make sense or may not be comparable in the new process. Be wary about changing measures, however; a change in measures is often used to obscure the poor performance of the new process. Thus a reconsideration of the measurement system should be a last resort. It is better to develop strong performance measures, stick with them through the implementation of a new practice, and figure out why the practice is not delivering what the benchmarking study indicated it should.

In most cases, particularly if the benchmarking study is conducted well, the performance measures will show improvement. The new process needs to become institutionalized (that is, become the normal way of doing things), performance measures need to be monitored and tracked to ensure that the higher level of performance is sustained, and continual improvement principles need to be applied to improve the process.

11. Reevaluate and Start Anew

Successfully importing a best practice changes the way the organization does its work and frequently even changes its culture. A new best practice certainly changes the results obtained on performance measures (if it did not, it would not be a successful implementation). Over time the environment within which the practice operates changes, as does the competitive world outside the agency. Healthy benchmarking programs need to be monitored, assessed, and recalibrated periodically to determine the effects of all these changes on the best practice and to evaluate progress on benchmarking goals and objectives.

Recalibration essentially means doing a mini-benchmarking study. The agency goes through all the steps of the methodology to understand its own new process, conducts a gap analysis, and identifies opportunities for performance improvement. Performance measures are reassessed, and the expected levels of performance on the measures are raised to account for the results achieved with the imported best practice. To the extent that the owners of the process keep up with the process, its performance measures, changes in the external competitive arena, and the rest of the information gathered in the original benchmarking study, the recalibration exercise requires less time and fewer resources. The ultimate goal is to have benchmarking be a continual process in which recalibration is a standard operating practice rather than a special activity done every year or two.

Benchmarking is the continual search for best practices to improve organizational performance. As soon as an organization implements a best practice, the opportunity to improve that process exists. As practitioners gain greater experience, expertise, and confidence with benchmarking, they can widen the search for best practices to more diverse organizations and processes. There are no perfect practices; every process can stand improvement. Thus the search for best practices continues. The power, vitality, creativity, and performance that benchmarking can bring to an organization are limited only by its willingness to conduct the quest.

Use the checklist in Worksheet 4.1, in the Resources, for guidance when applying the traditional benchmarking method in your own organization.

EXAMPLES OF TRADITIONAL BENCHMARKING

As mentioned earlier there are numerous examples of traditional benchmarking in the public, private, and nonprofit sectors. It is helpful to review a couple of recent case studies to better illustrate this process.

Environmental Protection Agency

In November 2003, U.S. Environmental Protection Agency (EPA) deputy administrator Stephen L. Johnson requested a short-term, overall review of the Superfund program. This study, referred to as the 120-day study, resulted in a report with 108 recommendations on how to make the Superfund program more efficient (U.S. EPA, 2006). The report also defined benchmarking as a "continuous process of measuring product, services, and practices against a strong competitor or recognized industry leader." In response to this report the Office of Superfund Remediation and Technology Innovation (OSRTI) created a benchmarking and best practices steering committee to select a process for the benchmarking evaluation. The five members of the benchmarking team focused their efforts on exploring site-specific payroll charging (SSPC).

SSPC is important for all EPA staff supported by Superfund money, including the many full-time employees who work outside Superfund program offices. Tracking site-specific hours worked is important not only for cost recovery efforts but also for public accountability, staff management, and workload management.

The benchmarking team identified three primary objectives: (a) apply benchmarking evaluation techniques to the OSRTI regional and headquarters SSPC process; (b) identify best practices in SSPC; and (c) make recommendations and develop an initial implementation plan to improve the SSPC process based on evaluation findings. The benchmarking team attempted to accomplish these objectives through two key steps.

First, the team collected and reviewed regional SSPC data from fiscal years 2000 through 2004. These data focused on an analysis of available payroll charging data. Of the ten total regions, the four that represented consistently high and consistently low SSPC charges were selected for subsequent study and interviews. The benchmarking team also analyzed the data to identify any systemic causes for the variation in performance. Analysis of the data did indicate that personnel allocation across the different regional offices loosely correlated to the overall regional SSPC rates.

The second step was to conduct interviews with EPA regional and headquarters staff. Interviews with twenty-nine managers and twenty-four staff in the four regions were completed during a two-month period. An additional eleven managers and three staff members in OSRTI were also interviewed. Interviewees received the questions in advance of the interview and were provided with the SSPC data during the interviews.

The data analysis and interview process provided some clear conclusions for the benchmarking team. The team identified eight factors that appeared critical to improving SSPC rates. The eight factors ranged from training to management oversight to changing regional culture.

International City/County Management Association

In 1994, more than twenty city and county managers in the International City/County Management Association (ICMA), from the United States and Canada, created the Comparative Performance Measurement Consortium. The initial participating managers identified a "need for data and information that could be used as a basis for evaluating and comparing service delivery performance" (International City/County Management Association, 2007b). There are now over 180 city and county organizations participating in the ICMA Center for Performance Measurement (CPM). Overall CPM helps local government organizations in Canada and the United States collect and analyze service delivery performance data. For each of the participating cities or counties, ICMA provides data collection templates and annual reports. ICMA currently collects data and evaluates results for over a dozen local government services, ranging from public safety to library services. One key element of the CPM is to create *apples-to-apples* comparisons across jurisdictions. This requires carefully defining the data or measures and a consistent data collection process (see Exhibit 4.1).

In the last decade ICMA's involvement in performance measurement has resulted in a number of success stories. Some cities used the measures to identify areas for improvements, thus increasing efficiency through internal evaluation. Others used the data to identify and foster great benchmarking partnerships. Few

---

Exhibit 4.1
How the CPM Accomplishes Its Mission

Defines indicators of effective service delivery.

Collects "apples-to-apples" comparative data from participating jurisdictions on these indicators and gives participants access to the full data sets.

Ensures a consistent set of data definitions among participating jurisdictions (as developed by participating jurisdictions).

Employs a rigorous data-cleaning process to ensure the integrity of the data and other information (using both computer models and ICMA staff review and oversight).

Facilitates analysis and discussions among program participants to determine the management practices key to communities in which data indicate high performance. This is accomplished via Web-based discussions on the private portion of the CPM Web site as well as face-to-face discussions among participating jurisdictions.

Collects "best practices/effective practices" as to the ways in which jurisdictions are using the data in their budgeting as well as financial/program planning processes.

Source: International City/County Management Association, 2007a.

of the success stories, however, rival the partnership between Golden, Colorado, and Veliko-Turnovo, Bulgaria.

Through the program CityLinks, run by the ICMA and funded by the U.S. Agency for International Development (USAID), Golden, Colorado, and Veliko-Turnovo, Bulgaria, were selected to be sister city organizations. CityLinks created an opportunity for the government staff of these two cities to collaborate and share information. One of the best results of this benchmarking is Veliko-Turnovo's improved infrastructure management. According to a recent ICMA performance management report the program greatly improved Veliko-Turnovo's ability to meet infrastructure demands and to increase its individual sustainability.

Using a performance based approach to infrastructure investment, Golden's public works director convinced the mayor of Veliko-Turnovo that resurfacing roads on a regular schedule, instead of waiting until the roads deteriorated, would save the city money. Based on Golden's experience, every U.S. dollar invested in preventive maintenance saved the city US$5 to later rebuild a road. Since adopting this approach and realizing the associated savings, Veliko-Turnovo has been able to secure targeted grants and bank financing to address additional infrastructure issues.

—**International City/County Management Association, 2004**

Veliko-Turnovo has now become a benchmarking city for a number of other Bulgarian cities. The infrastructure management approach that Veliko-Turnovo adopted from Golden is now starting to benefit these other cities. Meeting the goal of individual sustainability now means that Veliko-Turnovo has the staff expertise to be an industry leader for neighboring communities.

Golden, Colorado, benefited from this partnership as well. Although Golden did not directly implement any best or promising practices, it did improve its data collection and analysis in its role as a partnering organization. A more significant benefit for Golden was the lesson its government learned about the value of a commitment to achieve goals. The achievements of Veliko-Turnovo are an example to all organizations considering benchmarking—somewhere there is a solution to even the most daunting challenges.

The one lesson I will continue to reinforce to my staff and colleagues [is] we can't accept saying "we can't." Veliko-Turnovo has taught us that even the most difficult or challenging policy problem can be solved.

—Dan Hartman, public works director, Golden, Colorado
(personal communication, July 24, 2007)

Mineral Management Service (MMS) of the DOI

At the request of former Mineral Management Service (MMS) director Cynthia Quartman, the MMS Office of Policy and Management Improvement (PMI) created a benchmarking study of five royalty management programs in four states (Louisiana, New Mexico, Texas, and Wyoming). The objectives of the 1997 study were to describe and compare the four states' royalty programs to the MMS's royalty management program (RMP) and to identify state best practices for potential MMS adoption.

The MMS, an agency of the U.S. Department of the Interior (DOI), created a benchmarking study team of five individuals drawn from PMI, RMP, and the State and Tribal Royalty Auditing Committee. The team's benchmarking approach consisted of four key steps. First, the team members researched internal and external previous studies of state royalty management systems. Second, they closely evaluated data and information on each RMP. Third, they created a comprehensive survey to be administered in each state in the benchmarking study. The survey attempted to categorize data so as to enable apples-to-apples comparisons. Following the administration of the survey, the team members visited each state site. The fourth step in the process was to closely analyze the data. The data analysis created some challenges for the team, primarily because the state programs rarely matched up with the federal program.

The final study provided the MMS with considerable information on the variety of ways in which states manage their royalty management programs. The study also helped the MSS to categorize the different programs into seven distinct royalty management approaches. The final recommendation from the benchmarking team was for the MMS to consider the benchmarking report findings when working with states to develop royalty management program standards.

WARNINGS ABOUT TRADITIONAL BENCHMARKING

If a benchmarking team follows the eleven-step method, it is virtually guaranteed to find some best practices. Sometimes, however, teams get excited or distracted and end up not doing the job as well as could be expected. Teams need to be careful to avoid the following circumstances:

- *Engaging in industrial tourism:* carrying out a site visit without adequate preparation and thus failing to take home best practices
- *Engaging in self-deception:* having the belief that the benchmarking organization that has reviewed performance over time is already performing at an acceptable level
- *Looking for shortcuts:* skipping or adjusting steps in a way that is detrimental to the project
- *Permitting project delays:* allowing day-to-day problems to supersede the benchmarking project
- *Succumbing to impediments to implementation:* getting involved in politics, red tape, funding issues, or other factors that delay implementation of best practices and return on the investment
- *Becoming data heads:* becoming engrossed by data collection and unable to move ahead without additional analysis

Industrial Tourism

Often a simple site visit or mere comparison is confused with benchmarking. A simple review of a site visitation or a couple of Excel spreadsheets of data do not get an organization closer to implementing best practices or taking the necessary steps for management improvements. A recent experience illustrated this potential pitfall.

One of the authors was invited on a benchmarking visit to one of the most experienced and successful benchmarking companies in the world. The benchmarking team members, from a federal agency, appeared to have made all the necessary site visit preparations, including meeting as a team. They appeared to have done their preparation flawlessly; their enthusiasm was high, and their expectations were even higher.

After arriving and trading pleasantries with their hosts, the team members settled down to a discussion of the process for which their agency was seeking a best practice. As the hosts asked more and more penetrating questions, the team members had fewer and fewer substantive answers. It soon became clear that they were unprepared for a productive site visit with an experienced benchmarking partner. The trip ended with no best practices, few ideas for improvement, and an embarrassed benchmarking team.

This team suffered from the *industrial tourist* syndrome. Like tourists everywhere, team members had planned a visit, coordinated an itinerary, and visited all the top tourist attractions—but they left with little more than some warm memories to bring home. Industrial tourism (also referred to as *stop-and-shop* benchmarking) occurs when a team approaches a partner without the benefit of adequate research or an understanding of its own processes, hoping simply to pick and choose a few improvements.

Benchmarking is not industrial tourism, nor is it alchemy, miraculously turning the lead in your agency into gold. It is not yet a science, but it is more than an art. What separates benchmarking from tourism is the formal, structured process that organizations go through in their search for best practices. The more closely and accurately an organization follows the formal methodology, the more likely it is to find and import best practices successfully.

Self-Deception About Current Performance

As effective as benchmarking is when performed correctly, misuse of the method is possible. Companies have undertaken benchmarking programs that bear little or no resemblance to a search for best practices. Using a predefined set of measures, these firms crunch numbers to compare their performance with that of compatible firms and end up merely revealing their firm's relative rank within the comparison group. Ironically, good results on such indicators tend to discourage managers from striving for excellence (Doades, 1992). "We are already better than most others," they say, "so why do we need to improve?" This is a self-deception trap. An organization that finds itself at or near the top after such data analysis and decides to rest on its laurels is lulling itself into a sense of false security and will soon be overtaken by those it rated lower.

Shortcuts

To avoid many of the problems that can be encountered in benchmarking and to identify best practices to import, it is imperative that organizations adopt a methodology and then adhere to it. Just as measurement is the process of assigning numbers to something according to a defined set of rules, benchmarking is the process of searching for best practices according to a defined set of rules. The rules are defined by the method used. Think of the benchmarking methodology as analogous to a favorite recipe. If you choose to skip a step or substitute an ingredient, you may end up with a big problem. Skip cooking the potatoes for potato salad and no one will eat it. An inexperienced chef could accidentally use salt for sugar in a cookie recipe. After all, the texture and color are remarkably similar. The results, again, would be inedible.

Organizations and individuals that have some experience with benchmarking are in a different position. The experience they have gained from an initial project should be parlayed into another one. After all, benchmarking is about continuous improvement so why not apply the concept to the benchmarking process itself? An experienced cook often adjusts a recipe to accommodate personal tastes. If cookies are your favorite, you can substitute nuts for chocolate chips and still have a great cookie.

Project Delays

The formal, analytical steps in benchmarking create a few hurdles for benchmark teams and participating organizations. Sometimes these hurdles delay a project for months or years; at other times the hurdles end the benchmarking project entirely.

The first significant challenge to the traditional benchmarking methodology is its time-consuming and labor-intensive nature. The formal steps require significant staff time as team members review organizational goals, identify benchmark partners, identify measures and indicators, and collect data. For a traditional benchmarking process to be effective it must receive a high-priority emphasis from the organization. Often even a high-priority benchmarking project is shelved due to a more immediate crisis or a lack of resources.

Impediments to Implementation

Benchmarking is useful only when it is coupled with a willingness to take action. However, the implementation is the most difficult step. Benchmarking teams, like all groups, are subject to political influences that can prevent certain best practices from being adopted. Organizations may become frustrated with the traditional benchmarking approach, having spent weeks or months collecting data only to have this information ignored or marginalized.

Data Heads

Another often-cited challenge to this traditional approach is the likelihood of a benchmarking team's becoming bogged down in the data collection phase. Data collection can require a significant amount of time, effort, and concentration on detail (to define measures, standards, and indicators, for example). Although data collection is essential to the benchmarking process, it is not the end result. Yet at times organizations fall into the trap of creating a process for data collection and not a process for searching out and implementing best practices.

An organization that thoughtfully selects a process to benchmark can avoid these common mistakes. Once that selection has been made, one of the most difficult parts of benchmarking is completed, and the organization is ready to start on the exciting, energizing, and educational phase of the effort. Over the next few months, it will clearly define the process, measure its performance, select benchmarking partners, and come to understand their processes. As with any journey, the route one selects determines what one experiences and learns, the length and expense of the trip, the obstacles or detours encountered, and ultimately whether the destination is reached.

Organizations have also often adapted to overcome all these potential obstacles by executing a more streamlined benchmarking approach. This approach has been especially prevalent in the nonprofit sector but has also been used recently by government organizations. We define this streamlined approach as a solution-driven method, and we discuss it in the next chapter.

SUMMARY

- The traditional benchmarking methodology draws on the corporate model.
- This process emphasizes formal detailed sequential steps.
- The traditional method requires a careful analysis of measures and indicators for evaluation.
- The traditional method is often time consuming and can be labor intensive.
- The traditional method has been adapted by some organizations to a more streamlined approach.

The Solution-Driven Benchmarking Method

In keeping with the idea that benchmarking is a way to continuously improve performance, it seems only appropriate that the benchmarking methodology itself needed to be streamlined and enhanced. The traditional method was simply too costly for many organizations, especially those with pressing problems that could not wait four to six months for a resolution. As with many things, necessity was the parent of invention.

The research completed for this edition could not pinpoint a single organization or circumstance in which the solution-driven method first emerged. We attempted to fully document and consider the solution-driven steps, but they may yet be evolving. Our purpose is to report what we have observed in hopes that others will continue to replicate the solution-driven method, document its strengths and challenges, and report results to the performance improvement community at large.

When developing the solution-driven steps we were careful to compare these steps to problem-solving models as well as the traditional benchmarking approach. We found enough distinction among the steps to warrant treating them as a separate methodology. As the solution-driven approach evolves further it may merge with other methods. For now, we believe it is sufficiently distinct and successful that we can recommend it to others.

The solution-driven method was developed deductively. Individuals and organizations were using solution-driven steps without recognizing that they were in fact following a systematic method of comparing and improving performance. This is somewhat the reverse of the traditional approach, where the decision to benchmark is deliberative, and steps are clearly defined and followed. As we investigated the solution-driven approach we identified consistencies and trends that we generalized to the solution-driven method. Before 2006, no one began by saying, "I want to use a solution-driven approach to benchmarking." Our strongest hope for this book is that it will offer organizations a new way to benchmark. We encourage readers to capitalize on our research and the case examples by following the steps laid out in this chapter.

SNAPSHOT OF THE SOLUTION-DRIVEN METHOD

Recall from Chapter Three, "Preparing for Benchmarking," that solution-driven benchmarking is a streamlined method that is more like the gold rush than a treasure hunt and more like speed dialing than using a rotary dial. It depends on one or two individuals rather than a team and is not restricted to process analysis. People can use the solution-driven benchmarking method in solving problems or even in creating programs or processes where none previously existed.

At the heart of the solution-driven method is the network of professionals and organizations that the benchmarker can tap for promising practices. The search for best practices is conducted through these networks and the Internet and does not require site visits. Moreover, solution-driven benchmarking can be completed in several days or a few weeks, with follow-up conducted only as needed.

STEPS IN THE SOLUTION-DRIVEN METHOD

The solution-driven method is easy to follow and is dependent on one or two key individuals, not a team, for its completion. We describe the steps in Exhibit 5.1.

1. Discover the Problem

Before improvements or changes can be made, someone must first discover and define a problem. This discovery happens in a variety of ways. For example, a crisis, such as the destruction caused by Hurricane Katrina, can force public sector managers to recognize and acknowledge a problem that previously went unnoticed at their level. Or a previously recognized problem can reach a crisis proportion that leads to focused efforts to improve. Water or power shortages, for example, sometimes lead to conservation actions where none had previously been taken. In other circumstances a process, product, or service that has never before been offered may now be provided. The problem is figuring out how to do it. We offer several case examples that will illustrate the solution-driven benchmarking steps. But first, we want to finish describing all the steps. To complete step 1 in the solution-driven benchmarking method, ask yourself these questions:

- How do I know this problem exists?

- What evidence defines its boundaries?

- Is this problem under my control?

- Does fixing this problem require a substantial amount of resources?

- If I don't fix this problem, is my organization at risk? Am I at risk?

- Do I need to find a quick solution?

- Do I have a sense that others may have encountered this problem before?

- What measures or indicators tell me this is a serious problem?

2. Establish Criteria for the Solution

The persons using this method should have a very clear picture of what organizational life would be like without this problem. They should not expect simply to know the right result when they see it. Ask yourself these questions:

- What measures would demonstrate the problem was assuaged or eliminated?

- Have I noticed other organizations that have performed well in this area?

- What convincing evidence would illustrate that another person or organization has already addressed this issue or performance problem?

- What motivating factors ensure that solving this problem is worth the investment we would have to make to do so?

3. Search for Promising Practices

The search for promising practices is carried out by accessing such resources as professional and personal networks and the Internet. This is the step that most clearly defines the solution-driven model. One or more individuals access all available information. With the aid of professional associations, personal contacts, the Internet, and other local and international resources, these individuals explore the world for best or promising practices. As a benchmarker, you will ask your potential sources of a best practice these questions:

- Did you experience a problem or challenge similar to ours?

- How did you solve the problem?

- How much improvement or change did you note?

- What evidence is available that links the best practice with the improvement?

- Does the evidence demonstrating a successful best practice match the criteria we have established for our success?

- What was unique about your circumstances?

4. Implement Promising Practices

The next step in the solution-driven approach is to implement the best or promising practice that you have identified and are importing. Ask yourself these questions:

- Who needs to be involved in implementation?
- Do I have full authority to implement the best practice?
- Do I have a baseline of measures to serve as the point of comparison after implementation?
- Do I need additional research to implement this practice?

5. Monitor Progress

The last step in the solution-driven method is based on the philosophy of continuous improvement. The benchmarker needs to know whether the promising practice led to results. This step may be the most overlooked step because people like to assume the change has had a positive impact and do not like to face evidence to the contrary. Ask yourself these questions:

- Has the problem resurfaced? If so, is it in the same form?
- Have staff or volunteers embraced the change?
- What evidence demonstrates success?
- Do I need to keep monitoring this problem?

Completing Worksheet 5.1 will guide you through implementing the solution-driven benchmarking method in your own organization. Completing Worksheet 5.2 will help you identify your sources for best or promising practices. Both worksheets are in the Resources in the back of the book.

EXAMPLES OF SOLUTION-DRIVEN BENCHMARKING

Now that we have described all the steps, we offer several case examples to illustrate this methodology.

Guam Department of Administration

Early in our research we discovered Lourdes Perez, director of the Department of Administration of the Government of Guam. Guam Governor Felix Camacho appointed Perez shortly after his election in 2002. She took the helm at a time of fiscal crisis and spent much of her time trying to marshal enough cash to make the biweekly government payroll and manage grants and other funds in a way that ensured accounting procedures were followed. She also had to address numerous audit exceptions in the Government of Guam's financial statements.

Her efforts provide a clear and simple example of our solution-driven benchmarking method. She told us: "One of the recurring audit exceptions on our financial statements had to do with our chart of accounts. First, we had too many accounts and it was difficult to keep track of them all. Second, we weren't using many of them, or they were opened for a one-time entry and never used again. And we couldn't seem to balance them all. It was a real nightmare. I knew if I ever wanted to have a clean audit I needed to fix the chart of accounts."

Without knowing it Perez had completed the first two steps in solution-driven benchmarking. She had reviewed numerous audit exceptions and noticed that the chart of accounts was the root cause of several of those exceptions. She had clearly discovered and defined the problem. Second, the criteria for a successful solution had become obvious. Successful implementation of a best practice would result in the finding of no audit exceptions related to the chart of accounts.

Perez's search for promising practices began and ended a few short weeks after the discovery of the problem. At the time, Perez was serving as president of the Island Government Finance Officers Association (IGFOA), whose members include the finance officers and treasurers of the governments of the U.S. insular areas of Guam, the Commonwealth Northern Mariana Islands, the U.S. Virgin Islands, and American Samoa. Each year the IGFOA members attend the annual Government Finance Officers Association (GFOA) conference held in June on the U.S. mainland and then hold their own meeting immediately after this conference. During both the conference and meeting Perez searched high and low for ways to consolidate her chart of accounts. Although this may seem an easy task to an accountant, the problem had been building over a period of time and had become quite complex. In addition, several related policy issues had made it even more challenging. Perez sought information at the GFOA conference and queried her counterparts at the IGFOA meetings. She completed an effective search for best and promising practices, collecting a list of these practices before she returned to Guam. She then moved on to the implementation (step 4).

It wasn't an easy task, but Perez set her staff to work. She provided them with her list of promising practices and engaged a consultant to help. Within a few months the chart of accounts had been cleaned up and organized. The next financial statement had no exceptions caused by problems with the chart of accounts.

The final step of monitoring progress will be easy for her. She has eliminated the root cause of many of the problems, and now only she can authorize the opening of new accounts. After three years there are still no audit exceptions related to the chart of accounts.

The solution-driven method helped me find realistic solutions to my problem.

—Lourdes Perez, Department of Administration,
Government of Guam

The lessons offered by this case study are simple. The government of Guam had a clearly defined problem whose resolution was urgent. An individual, Perez, used two professional networks to find promising practices used by others. As an administrator and political appointee she had many distractions, including giving legislative testimony, managing the funding of government operations, and supervising her staff. She did not become distracted by other fires in her life, however, even though there were many. And Perez recognized that other people probably had promising practices that could help her. Perhaps most important was that Perez used her leadership skills and the authority of her position to ensure long-term successful implementation.

Southern Utah Recycling Coalition

In January 2005, a small number of committed citizens formed the Southern Utah Recycling Coalition (SURC), whose mission is to promote recycling and awareness throughout a five-county region in southern Utah. SURC submitted a grant proposal to the U.S. EPA, which awarded SURC $41,000 to help it accomplish several goals. One goal was to complete a waste stream analysis (WSA). The WSA would measure the amount of waste that could be recycled and focus public attention on the importance of recycling. Few of the SURC members had experience with conducting a WSA, and they quickly discovered they needed help. The problem of how to conduct a WSA had been recognized before the grant was made, and it came to the forefront shortly afterward. Step 1 in the solution-driven method, discover the problem, reached a crescendo after receiving the grant award.

SURC board members had two criteria for success (step 2)—measure recyclable waste in a way that met the grant requirements and gain the public's attention while doing so. They tossed around several potential WSA measures. For example, did they want to measure all recyclable waste placed in the landfill during a certain period of time or household waste only? How many hours, days, or weeks of waste must they examine? Would a sample from one day suffice? Did they have to resort to dumpster diving to conduct the waste stream analysis? The questions mounted.

Fortunately, SURC board members had already begun the search for promising practices. In preliminary discussions with the Recycling Coalition of Utah (RCU) and the EPA grant coordinator, they were advised to seek help from other, more established recycling operations that had already completed a WSA. A variety of names and sources of potential best practices had already been compiled but not used. After a struggle with other priorities and additional research on the approach, SURC members made a few contacts for advice. The results were outstanding.

SURC members decided to combine best practices from a number of sources to implement the WSA in Cedar City, Utah. With the help of volunteers and under the direction of Blue Sky Recycling of St. George, Utah, the WSA was successfully completed. Volunteers (students from Southern Utah University) were trained on how to identify and sort recyclable waste. The recyclables were weighed, bagged, and recycled through Blue Sky Recycling. The total weight of all the waste was then compared to the weight of the recyclables. The results suggested that about 40 percent of the waste collected from homes and businesses in the sample could be recycled. Equally important, the *Spectrum,* a daily newspaper for southern Utah, published a front-page article with pictures of the WSA process and students measuring and sorting the waste.

We really didn't know where to begin. Our solution-driven partners helped us launch our recycling program.

—Jenifer Harris, vice president of operations,
Southern Utah Recycling Coalition

The SURC experience provides another example of solution-driven benchmarking with some unique lessons learned. First, this method can be used for a one-time problem or circumstance. SURC members were not trying to improve a process conducted on a daily basis. They were attempting to do something they had never done before, which is lesson two. The solution-driven approach can help organizations to implement new procedures. Why struggle to create a process if an organization already has a promising practice to follow? A final lesson can be derived from SURC's experience. Although each step of the method was followed, the five steps were not necessarily completed sequentially. Identifying the performance measures that would be criteria for a successful solution (step 2) and the search for promising practices (step 3) were somewhat iterative. SURC members did not implement the promising practices (step 4) until they were confident of the results of steps 2 and 3. SURC continues to support recycling in southern Utah.

Graduate School, USDA, Executive Leadership Program

In March 2007, approximately 232 federal employees gathered in Cambridge, Maryland, for an Executive Leadership Program (ELP) workshop titled "High Performing Organizations: Benchmarking and More." During this four-day workshop, participants were divided into small groups and asked to conduct an abbreviated benchmarking study. The results were impressive and closely followed the solution-driven method's steps. Two teams' results were particularly noteworthy.

Snow Removal   The state of Pennsylvania received significant adverse media attention the week of March 5, 2007, due to extreme traffic jams during a snowstorm. A few of the ELP participants were either from Pennsylvania or had experienced the portion of the highway shut down by snow and immobilized cars. Out of curiosity and with sincere interest in learning about the problems of snow removal, these participants, calling themselves the Dirty Dozen, set about benchmarking snow removal. Step 1 in their solution-driven approach was to define the problem. The media had already done the job for them. The problem was slow or ineffective snow removal on Pennsylvania's interstate highways. The criterion for success was more timely snow removal in future snowstorms. (The Dirty Dozen also developed the IPOLO performance measure model described in Chapter Two as part of this activity.) After some research on the Internet and a few telephone calls, the team identified the Washington, D.C., Department of Public Works; the League of Minnesota Cities; and the Washington State Department of

Transportation (DOT) as having some promising practices for Pennsylvania. All these organizations had experienced similar traffic jams and snow removal problems during unexpected, significant snowfalls. What best practices were discovered? First, all of these partners had assigned one person to be a *snow czar,* to coordinate the efforts of numerous individuals and departments during heavy snowstorms. Pennsylvania did not have a snow czar when its crisis occurred. Additionally, the League of Minnesota Cities and the Washington State DOT provided a free text message service for drivers about road closures. This helped drivers prevent traffic jams by rerouting around some roads and staying current on weather and road conditions. Finally, the D.C., Minnesota, and Washington state partners had classified all roads by function, whereas Pennsylvania had not. These classifications helped drivers understand the emergency routes and aided the snow removal crews in prioritizing snowplows. The Dirty Dozen had now successfully completed the first three steps in the solution-driven method, demonstrating its ease and helpful results. Although none of the team members was in a position to recommend these changes to the governor of Pennsylvania (step 4), it is clear that Pennsylvania could easily follow this same method and identify promising practices for improved snow removal.

Placing Foster Children in Permanent Homes   The ELP group that called itself Team 22 Caliber defined its problem as children spending excessive time in foster care waiting for adoption in the Washington, D.C., area. This problem was particularly important to the team because one member had personal experiences with the D.C. adoption process. Measures clearly defined the problem, a current delay of 3.7 years and a criterion for success of placement in one year. Team 22 Caliber set about finding promising practices for the problem and elected to look at Richland County Children Services, Mansfield, Ohio, and the Los Angeles County Department of Children and Family Services, Los Angeles, California. These partners offered four best practices for consideration. First, establish a dual approval process for homes so foster care parents can easily adopt if and when such a decision is made. Second, establish community service teams to support foster caregivers. Third, provide free counseling services for families planning to adopt, and finally, assign one social worker for the life of the case. The partners had streamlined the placement process via these promising practices, and the team highly recommended that the D.C. placement agency consider them all.

These ELP workshop examples illustrate three important points. First, a clearly defined problem and criteria for success are critical prerequisites to the step 3 search for promising practices in the solution-driven approach. After clearly defining the problem and establishing measures for the solution, each team was able to focus its research time on specific issues. Second, with a small investment of time the Internet can yield an enormous amount of information. Third, the telephone still works. Web pages, articles, and other sources on the Internet frequently provide a contact name and telephone number for additional information. Some ELP team members called the partners and spoke to individuals about a promising practice. The training activity yielded tangible results for consideration by those responsible for a problem.

Layton, Utah

Another interesting case explores a situation faced by Alex Jensen, city manager of Layton, Utah. The city of Layton is located along a corridor between Salt Lake City and Ogden that is bounded by the Wasatch Range to the east and the Great Salt Lake to the west. Some people consider Layton a suburb of Salt Lake City because many of its residents commute south into the city to work or to attend one of several universities. Layton, like numerous other U.S. suburbs, was finding that the interstate highway serving it was becoming more and more congested. In 2001, the Utah Transit Authority (UTA) and the state of Utah began to explore implementing a commuter rail system to serve Layton and the communities to its north and south. Jensen and his city council were faced with an important decision—where to place the station for the rail line. This was the very beginning of the solution-driven method, discovery and definition of the problem, which was how to find the right location for the station.

Looking internally first, Jensen, the council, and their staff collected a list of criteria for success (step 2). The station had to have easy access to Interstate 15, the only interstate highway running north to Ogden, Utah, and to Idaho and south to Salt Lake City, southern Utah, and Nevada and Arizona. If rail passengers drove to the station from outside Layton, it was very likely they would arrive and depart via I-15. The location had to be acceptable to the public, provide adequate parking, and meet construction standards such as those for the width of the track. Also, the aesthetics needed to be consistent with the appearance of the surrounding community and acceptable to the public. This list represents complex and substantial requirements and is illustrative of common problems faced by growing cities.

Fortunately, Layton and its leaders were not alone. Layton staff and elected officials began an extensive research and networking process as part of the search for promising practices (step 3). They met with UTA staff transportation experts, state transportation personnel, and various elected officials to get ideas. They also met with managers and engineers employed by other cities in Salt Lake County to discuss how they had designed and developed other rail stations. Finally, they met with local business owners and queried the public at various points in the research.

Perhaps one of the more interesting aspects of the search involved Envision Utah, a public and private sector partnership created to help Utah achieve quality growth. Envision Utah sponsored several transit-oriented development workshops, one of which focused on Layton. The workshop included training on various aspects of the development, such as how to establish proper ordinances, how to ensure mixed-use development, and how to include walking and bike trails. Workshop participants created a variety of best practices for Layton to consider.

Layton also had the benefit of a dedicated and enthusiastic employee. Peter Matson, the city's long-range planner, was intimately involved in the rail project simply because of his position with the city, but he went beyond the call of duty when he took a personal trip to visit family in Oregon. On that trip he spent time riding commuter rail between Beaverton and Portland, Oregon. He photographed the stations and surrounding areas, studied the location and architecture of the stations, and went out of his way to gather information to present to Layton's city council. He created his own list of best practices and pooled them with those the city had gained from collaborating with Envision Utah, the local business owners, and the Layton community.

Layton officials seem very satisfied with the results to date. They selected a site that was appropriate and well supported by the community and the many people involved in the selection process. They have an architectural design that suits the Layton community, and they have established ordinances that support multi-use development in the area surrounding the station. Perhaps more important, in its 2006 budget the U.S. Federal Transit Administration awarded $80 million to support transit in Utah, part of which will help fund the Layton station. The first riders of this long-awaited and worthwhile rail project are expected in 2008.

Layton provides another unique example of the solution-driven benchmarking method. Unlike the processes described earlier, this entire process spanned several years. The first two steps, however, occurred rather quickly and clearly. The problem was discovered (step 1) and criteria were established (step 2) within a few months of the initial discussions. The search for promising practices (step 3) appeared to continue throughout the development project and even into the beginning of implementation. Layton's experience reinforces how important it is for organizations to complete those first two steps. They serve as continual touchstones for determining what is or is not a promising practice. If an idea did not contribute in some way to the established criteria, it was not considered further.

All the cases described here illustrate the flexibility and effectiveness of solution-driven benchmarking. If they piqued your interest you will enjoy reading Part Three, "Benchmarking in Sectors." In each of the upcoming chapters we discuss additional solution-driven benchmarking cases equally as intriguing as these.

COMMON SENSE OR METHODOLOGY?

What distinguishes the solution-driven benchmarking method from common sense or good management practices? Several things. First, solution-driven benchmarking has become the nexus between several management practices that have become so ingrained that managers and staff take them for granted. For example, before the TQM and reinventing government efforts, many organizations had an aversion to using an idea drawn from elsewhere. The phrase "not invented here" described their typical attitude; they would not even try to change something unless the idea to do so was internally generated. The term *continuous improvement* simply did not exist prior to the 1970s. Many organizations were loath to look outside their own expertise for better ideas or solutions to difficult problems. Now it is expected that public and nonprofit organizations will create cultures that focus on empowerment, continuous improvement, streamlining processes, productivity, strategic planning, and serving customers. This subtle but important organizational cultural change has fostered solution-driven benchmarking. In fact it has become common practice to look externally for ideas and solutions to problems, so common that people have failed to recognize and systematically document the practice. What might appear to be common sense is actually a method that has evolved along with management practices and organizations throughout the past two decades. Think of the solution-driven method as chicken soup or orange juice. For years mothers have followed their common sense and experience and have given their families chicken soup and orange juice to help prevent or overcome the common cold. Now science has proven that this practice is indeed effective. Similarly, people have been practicing solution-driven benchmarking because they got results. Now researchers are discovering the details behind it—how and why it works.

Additionally, the solution-driven approach can be distinguished from problem-solving models by its focus on comparisons and professional networks. Problem-solving methods usually include such steps as define the problem, analyze data, identify root causes, brainstorm solutions, and implement changes. Granted, problem solving and solution-driven benchmarking have a common goal—to change a difficult situation or circumstance into a more positive or beneficial one. However, problem solving (and traditional benchmarking) tends to spend more time and resources on analyzing the problem and getting to the root cause. Solution-driven benchmarking requires that more time be devoted to looking for others who have already solved the problem. It reaches immediately beyond the internal circumstances to look for solutions.

WARNINGS ABOUT THE SOLUTION-DRIVEN METHOD

We would be remiss if we did not point out some pitfalls in the solution-driven method. This benchmarking approach appears to be vulnerable in two areas. First, it does not require people to carry out an extensive analysis before launching a search for a promising practice. It may fail if the individuals involved do not have sufficient understanding of the problem to recognize the solution that will be a permanent fix, not just a Band-Aid.

Like its traditional counterpart, solution-driven benchmarking is also vulnerable during implementation. The best practice is only as good as the attention given to implementing it well. In spite of these warnings, a number of organizations are successfully discovering and implementing best or promising practices through this streamlined approach.

SUMMARY

- Solution-driven benchmarking is more streamlined and less complex than the traditional approach.

- Solution-driven benchmarking requires five steps: discover the problem, establish criteria for solutions, search for promising practices, implement promising practices, and monitor progress.

- Solution-driven benchmarking relies on the Internet, professional networks, and personal contacts as sources of solutions and partners.

- Organizations such as the Government of Guam; Graduate School, USDA; Southern Utah Recycling Coalition; and Layton, Utah, have successfully applied the solution-driven method.

- Solution-driven benchmarking is well integrated into the performance improvement culture.

- Solution-driven benchmarking is vulnerable to criticism because it does not require extensive data analysis.

PART THREE

Benchmarking in Sectors

G lobalization and performance improvement trends have changed the public's perspective on governments and nonprofits. Taxpayers and constituents now expect these organizations to deliver high-quality products and services at minimal cost. Fortunately, benchmarking is clearly seen as a tool that government and nonprofit organizations can use to find ways to enhance performance. As we researched benchmarking we discovered the importance of sharing the ways in which the various sectors used or adapted the methodology to their unique characteristics.

In Chapter Six, "Benchmarking in State and Local Governments," we give a historical overview of how the Oregon state government influenced benchmarking at the state and local government levels. We also discuss a survey of leaders' reasons for deciding to benchmark, and we link the results to several examples. Cases in North Carolina and Utah demonstrate that states and municipalities have sufficient size and resources to conduct traditional or solution-driven benchmarking studies. By using benchmarking, state and local governments have responded well to the external pressures to enhance performance.

We included Chapter Seven, "Benchmarking in Nonprofits," because we recognize the unique characteristics of nonprofit organizations. Case examples are drawn from large, small, local, and national nonprofit organizations and range from a children's museum to a food bank. We found improving performance is especially important to nonprofits when resources are shrinking or special projects are leading them to change.

We would be remiss if we did not share with you some of the many successful benchmarking studies that have taken place outside the United States. Chapter Eight, "Benchmarking in the International Community," presents examples ranging from Scotland to Guam and from tourism to footpaths. This chapter is evidence that benchmarking is truly an international phenomenon.

Benchmarking in State and Local Governments

Most municipal, county, and state governments are familiar with benchmarking. In fact nearly half of all U.S. cities collect performance measures for the purpose of benchmarking (Ammons, 2001; Poister & Streib, 1994, 1999). According to a recent study surveying 231 government executives worldwide (including managers from virtually all administrative service areas such as finance, human resources, and information technology), 73 percent of government executives are currently conducting benchmarking activities (Howard & Killmartin, 2006). The results of this study also show that of the small percentage currently not benchmarking, 69 percent said they were "very likely" or "somewhat likely" to begin using benchmarking in the near future.

These survey data support our sense from our own research that benchmarking has caught on nearly everywhere in the public sector, from the largest agencies in the federal government to the smallest towns in rural America. Even if they are simply asking, "How do we compare to our neighboring jurisdiction?" or, "Have we improved service delivery efficiency from last year?" local and state governments are using benchmarking both internally and externally to find best practices.

HISTORICAL OVERVIEW

Benchmarking came to the forefront in state and local governments in a slightly different way than it did in federal and nonprofit entities. The federal government was greatly influenced by the private sector and followed that sector's lead in the late 1980s and early 1990s by applying the traditional benchmarking method to process improvement. The federal government began benchmarking with the private sector first. Although state and local governments entered the benchmarking arena at about the same time, they followed their peers—other state and local governments—rather than mimicking the private sector. Several state governments followed the state of Oregon's lead and took a comprehensive look at outcomes and set benchmarks or standards for performance. Oregon emphasized partnerships among state agencies, local governments, the private sector, and citizen organizations but did not follow a specific benchmarking method. Other states selected key areas in which to apply the benchmarking method and promoted their success accordingly. At the local government level, Mayor Joe Sensenbrenner, of Madison, Wisconsin, became famous for implementing total quality management, including a small benchmarking component. But local governments tended to focus on results, such as finding best practices, instead of using benchmarks or benchmarking. For example, in 1995, the U.S. Conference of Mayors created and published a list of best practices that had been compiled simply by asking members to report them. Although they used a variety of approaches, by the early 1990s most states and cities were definitely in the game.

BENCHMARKING AND STATE GOVERNMENTS

Oregon was the first state to receive significant attention for its benchmarking effort, even though this effort did not really involve what we have defined as benchmarks and benchmarking:

> *A benchmark is a standard or point of comparison.*

> *Benchmarking is a methodology used to improve performance by finding high-performing organizations and importing their practices to the home organization.*

In 1991, Oregon published a list titled "Oregon Benchmarks: Setting Measurable Standards for Progress," which was presented to the Oregon Legislature

(Oregon Progress Board, 1991). It consisted of performance standards linked to the state's strategic goals, and given our definitions (which we have just reiterated), we would agree to call them benchmarks. Oregon took a bold step forward by setting and publishing these performance standards and has been widely recognized for doing so.

Oregon's state agencies used these benchmarks as a way to focus improvement efforts, and much has been written about their successes. However, little has been written about the process that the agencies underwent to find specific goals and to attain those successes. Because the methods Oregon agencies followed have not been made clear, others cannot assume that they followed a traditional benchmarking methodology. Much to Oregon's credit, though, benchmarks remain a cornerstone of the state's performance reporting, despite numerous changes in the administration.

Oregon's approach is unique in two ways. First, the benchmarks evolved from desired outcomes or goals that would improve the state's society and the quality of life for its citizens (an objective that we discuss in more detail later in this chapter). Performance reporting is constructed around these long-term goals yet includes typical output measures such as work completed, customer satisfaction, quality, and cycle time. Oregon truly provides a wonderful example of the right way to measure long-term goals and interim performance. At the same time, because the state has not promoted benchmarking as a method of finding ways to improve, we cannot say that Oregon conducts benchmarking studies.

Other states attempted to follow Oregon's lead, but their efforts collapsed. For example, Connecticut, Florida, and Maine followed suit by creating a legislature-mandated benchmark system remarkably similar to Oregon's. These efforts failed largely due to changes in the administration and in the management structure of the benchmark reporting process.

Second, Oregon focused its efforts on performance and on forming coalitions among communities, various government agencies, and the private sector. The Oregon legislature created a *progress board* to manage the partnership and improvement process and to receive the performance reports. Few states have the executive and legislative leadership structure and political will to orchestrate such a large undertaking. Oregon was clearly a forerunner in states' efforts to benchmark even though it did not appear to rely on traditional benchmarking methods. We greatly admire its accomplishments and offer its efforts as a unique model for any organization that wants to improve performance.

As shown in Oregon's efforts, coalitions are an important part of benchmarking in state and local governments, and both national and local associations have played an important role in assisting to build community coalitions. National associations have become important in helping to organize and facilitate a number of benchmarking studies. Associations such as the National Association of State Auditors, Comptrollers and Treasurers; National Conference of State Legislatures; National League of Cities; and the U.S. Conference of Mayors provide opportunities for their member organizations to share information and to discover potential benchmarking partners. Additionally, many of these national associations make an extra effort to recognize performance leaders who provide best practices to their member organizations or individuals.

WHY STATE AND LOCAL GOVERNMENTS PURSUE BENCHMARKING

The goal of benchmarking for the private sector is to manage and produce more efficiently to increase profits. The goal for public sector entities is not quite as straightforward—state and local governments have numerous reasons to pursue benchmarking and may pursue multiple goals with their benchmarking endeavors. However numerous the reasons, these goals can be reduced to four or five general categories.

Most commonly, officials cite wanting to improve productivity or efficiency and accountability. In the survey mentioned earlier, government executive respondents were asked to rank their benchmarking goals by importance (Howard & Killmartin, 2006). The results reflect the same goals that we hear continually while participating in federal or local government benchmarking projects. The ranking order is as follows:

1. Improve productivity or efficiency (79 percent)

2. Increase customer or user satisfaction (70 percent)

3. Improve accountability and transparency (59 percent)

4. Increase employee satisfaction, loyalty, and motivation (52 percent)

5. Improve technology utilization (47 percent)

6. Complete transformation of functions (36 percent)

Each of these goals provides compelling reasons to benchmark, but in the following discussion, we will focus on efficiency, customer satisfaction, and greater accountability or transparency.

Efficiency

Efficiency is a fundamental goal for many benchmarking projects. There is no question that improving an organization's efficiency requires some degree of performance measurement. In both municipal and state government organizations, numerous areas can be improved by better efficiency. The quest for efficiency in local government is often driven by two pressures: limited financial resources and citizen satisfaction. Benchmarking projects that identify best practices can benefit local government in both these areas.

An excellent example of a benchmarking program that focuses on improving efficiency is the Mandatory Performance Measurement Program (MPMP), implemented in 2000 for the more than four hundred municipalities in Ontario, Canada, including the two largest cities, Toronto and Ottawa. This program targets twelve core service areas ranging from general government to wastewater to parks. Within these twelve service areas, municipalities are required to annually report their "effectiveness" and "efficiency" across fifty-four measures. As municipalities report their annual operating costs for each service area, inefficiencies are noted as well as best practices. The data collected through the Ontario MPMP project have led to establishment of the Ontario Centre for Municipal Best Practices (OCMBP) partnership (Burke, 2005).

The purpose of the OCMBP partnership between the Ontario municipal governments and provincial government is to "support the evolution of performance measurement for Ontario municipalities by reviewing and analyzing performance data to identify best practices" (Ontario Centre for Municipal Best Practices, 2007). The OCMBP prepares reports offering guidance for practitioners interested in applying these best practices. Since 2002, OCMBP has noted a number of best practices for various policy areas: roads, transit, waste management, and water or sewer services. Many of these best practices have been specifically aimed toward efficiency improvements.

For example, Hamilton, the third largest city in Ontario, improved the efficiency of its transit system through the use of universal transit passes targeted to university students. In 2001, the Hamilton Street Railway (HSR) sold the universal pass to students for CAN$58 per semester, a savings over the $46 per month regular student fare. As a result, Hamilton increased ridership among the university students by up to 45 percent. This increase in student ridership increased overall transit efficiency in several ways. First, it allowed HSR to capitalize on spare capacity in the system and to carry a portion of the new riders at no or little cost. This new ridership increased revenue by CAN$500,000. Hamilton Street Railway incurred additional costs due to adding routes near universities, but the universal pass program still generated more revenue than expense. Now, the universal pass for students is built into the fees for many students at the different universities in Hamilton. This prepayment process has continued to increase revenue and to decrease the administrative costs of issuing passes. This HSR program has been noted as a best practice by the OCMBP (2004) and has now been implemented by other communities with a large student population, such as Toronto (University of Toronto) and Kingston (Queen's University). The practice is also being extended beyond university student riders to large private companies with large numbers of potential transit patrons.

Customer Satisfaction

Increasing customer satisfaction is also a key purpose for conducting benchmarking projects. Since the publication of Osborne and Gaebler's book *Reinventing Government: How the Entrepreneurial Spirit Is Transforming the Public Sector* (1992), the notion of treating taxpayers as customers has been widespread throughout the public sector, even though the effectiveness of this perspective is still being debated (Kettl, 1998; Moe, 1994; Pegnato, 1997; Thompson, 2000). Yet the reality is that many services provided by local governments operate very much like a business. For example, many municipal airports, water treatment facilities, and sewer plants now operate like businesses. A recent benchmarking project led by the American Water Works Association Research Foundation (AwwaRF) illustrates using benchmarking to attain this goal of improving customer satisfaction.

The AwwaRF is a "member-supported, international, nonprofit organization that sponsors research to enable water utilities, public health agencies, and other service professions to provide safe and affordable drinking water to consumers" (American Water Works Association Research Foundation, 2007). In 2006, AwwaRF organized a benchmarking project—culminating in a report titled *Benchmarking Water Utility Customer Relations Best Practices*—in which over fifteen municipal water authorities participated. These participants represented most regions of the United States and included, for example, the Louisville Water Company, City of Phoenix Water Services Department, Long Beach Water Department, and City of Cleveland Division of Water. These benchmarking participants identified three principal objectives:

1. Identify customer relations best practices from other relevant organizations;
2. Identify metrics for both internal performance tracking and external comparison;
3. Develop tools that enable water utilities to improve customer relation [Patrick & Kozlosky, 2006].

Results from the project conclusively show that water utility companies can provide high levels of customer service and can do it efficiently. Results from the AwwaRF research also show that the top-performing cities used specific best practices. For example, virtually all the top participants with high marks in meter maintenance allowed their field employees to go directly to job sites from their homes and provided them with cell phones to improve communication. Overall the top-performing organizations treated their employees as well as the employees are expected to treat their customers. Each of these best practices improves customer service, and illustrates local government turning to benchmarking to enhance customer satisfaction.

A number of local government entities have stressed the notion of giving their citizens value for their tax dollars. This "value for tax dollars" mantra is similar to the emphasis on giving customers their money's worth found among private sector business owners. Business owners value the opinions of satisfied customers and see these customers as the best type of marketing campaign—and they try to avoid situations that lead a customer to say, "It was OK, but not worth the money." State and local leaders often approach their service delivery responsibilities the same way, asking, for example: "Do we spend taxes on roads or parks?" "What policy areas are of the highest importance to our citizens?" And, "How can we efficiently stretch each tax dollar to maximize its value?" Pleasing citizens—like satisfying customers—can be a tall order, but one that is definitely achievable. Many government entities have tried to accomplish this endeavor by making their budgets more open and accessible, so citizens can more easily express their peferences. This leads to the next objective we will discuss, greater accountability and transparency.

Enhancing and improving customer satisfaction is an important responsibility of local government officials. In my twenty years working with municipal governments I've seen the concept [of] "giving citizens their money's worth" really take hold—largely through cities sharing ideas and collaborating solutions in overcoming this challenge of communicating the budget process to citizens.

—Ken Bullock, executive director, Utah League of Cities and Towns (personal communication, May 7, 2007)

Greater Accountability or Transparency

Managers in top-performing organizations at both the state and local levels insist on accountability from their subordinates and expect to be held to the same accountability by their superiors (Ammons, 2001). This internal accountability is one force driving organizations to monitor and report data measures tracking performance and productivity. In addition to being held internally accountable, government employees have a significant responsibility to be accountable to taxpayers. This accountability begins with government entities spending tax dollars efficiently and expending resources that produce the benefits or services demanded by the public. Transparency is often the key to government entities' becoming more accountable. It is difficult for the general public to approve or disapprove of a government entity's expenditure if it is buried in a complex budget document.

To illustrate, Cumberland County, Pennsylvania, recently received the Fiscal Accountability and Best Management Practices award from the Pennsylvania Governor's Center for Local Government Services. Cumberland County received the award for revamping its budget document to make it easier to communicate to the general public and to increase the use of the budget document as an internal management tool. The document now gives the reader (or citizen) an overview of services provided by each office, plus a description of how these services fit into the overall vision of the county (Pennsylvania Department of Community and Economic Development, 2007).

It's all about making sure we are managing taxpayers' dollars for the best results, [it] transforms the budget process and documentation. It communicates clear directions for our County, and makes this huge financial document more constituent-friendly and open. It is the cornerstone of our efforts to add greater focus and accountability for results in County operations.

—Cumberland County commissioner Gary Eichelberger,
describing the county's innovative budget document
(Cumberland County, Pennsylvania, 2007)

This example illustrates how the objective of greater accountability or transparency can be achieved. The responsibility for heightened accountability to and transparency for citizens is a key function of effective government organizations, from the federal government to agencies in the smallest towns. We will address this issue of accountability in greater depth in Chapter Nine.

The other three goals found in Howard and Killmartin's (2006) international government executives survey (increase employee satisfaction, improve technology utilization, and complete transformation of functions or processes), are often not pursued separately. As illustrated by the Awwa Research Foundation's benchmarking study, frequently these goals can be blended and achieved through the same benchmarking project. When city water departments improved employee satisfaction, customer satisfaction improvements quickly followed. The final goal mentioned on this list, transformation of functions, seems to occur most frequently in the midst of large-scale changes. Often this can be the result of newly elected officials or new senior managers who are looking to consolidate, expand, or streamline a service output. This top-down administrative change can lead to benchmarking to completely transform functions.

WHO SHOULD PARTICIPATE IN A BENCHMARKING PROJECT?

We have discussed some of the reasons for government organizations to venture down the benchmarking path, but before this journey begins, a state or local government entity must evaluate which stakeholders to include. The question of whom to involve in a benchmarking project is more serious for public agencies than it is for private sector organizations. A benchmarking project in the private sector that is well supported internally is unlikely to be affected by any outside forces. This is not the case in the public sector, where both internal and external influences must be considered at the beginning of the project because typically a great variety of groups, individuals, and situations have the potential to derail any public sector benchmarking project.

This public scrutiny gives rise to the following questions: "What are the reasons for spending time and energy to get others involved?" "Who should be involved?" "What will these people contribute?" "At what point in the project's timeline is their participation important?" The more thought that is given to these questions, the greater the likelihood that support for the project will be widespread. Thinking through these questions will also help to ensure that the project is based on identified customer needs rather than on the personal agendas of politicians and other forces in the political community.

Several significant benefits accrue to an organization that involves all appropriate stakeholders in the benchmarking project:

1. The organization will have a broader perspective on what is important to its overall functioning and an indication of the most valuable results.

2. The increased internal and external support will help drive the project through to completion.

3. The commitment to long-term success will be greater because people feel involved.

4. The organization will be able to draw from the technical or substantive knowledge held by a variety of people.

5. The organization will be practicing good leadership, management, and communication principles.

6. The project results will be more reliable and valid.

The following examples illustrate a variety of efforts to involve stakeholders. The North Carolina benchmarking project, municipal resort community project, and Utah benchmarking project are all great examples that successfully followed key steps to build a benchmarking team and begin a benchmarking study.

North Carolina Benchmarking Project: Forming a Broad Coalition

The North Carolina Benchmarking Project (NCBP), initiated in 1995, is a positive example of how local governments can create a broad coalition and improve opportunities to share data and measure performance. The goal of this project has been to allow participating municipalities to compare themselves with each other and to make comparisons of their own internal operations over time. As a result North Carolina has achieved many of the previously mentioned benefits of benchmarking.

Seventeen municipalities participate in this benchmarking project. Their benchmarking process includes compiling service and cost information, cleaning the data for accuracy, calculating the selected performance measures, and comparing the results (UNC [University of North Carolina] School of Government, North Carolina Benchmarking Project, 2007). This program has been very successful, primarily due to the large collaborative efforts of the North Carolina Municipal League, the School of Government at the University of North Carolina-Chapel Hill, the North Carolina Government Finance Officers Association, the North Carolina Association of County Commissioners, and the North Carolina Local Government Budget Association. In 2006, the NCBP produced its ninth annual report.

Now the data collection and sharing for the NCBP operates like clockwork:

- August: distribution of service profile and accounting forms
- October: data collection deadline
- November: distribution of performance and cost data
- December: data cleaning meeting
- January: first draft of performance and cost data report
- January: final version of performance and cost data report

This process has been repeated year after year since 1995. Although significant staff and leadership work is required for each of these annual phases, often much of the heavy lifting in benchmarking comes in the early stages. Once a benchmarking project reaches a point where it is sustained by broad, stable organizations (such as the NCBP participants mentioned earlier), it becomes more credible and therefore more routine. However, we emphasize again—getting to this point is not easy.

Two key strengths of the NCBP reflect items 2 and 4 in the previous list of the benefits of involving many stakeholders:

- Having both internal and external support from others helps drive the project through to completion each year.

- Having a broad coalition creates the opportunity to draw from the technical and substantive knowledge held by a variety of people.

Resort Community Benchmarking Group: Choosing Partners with Similar Composition

Benchmarking can provide meaningful results for partners who appear to have little in common (remember the example of L.L. Bean and Xerox in Chapter One); however, frequently, organizations seek partners who are similar in composition. The Resort Community Benchmarking Group, established in 2006, reflects this desire to find partners that offer an apples-to-apples comparison. For example, the government of Park City, Utah, a popular resort community, faces a number of atypical management tasks. Because of this, a limited number of municipalities provide a close comparison. Park City's population is around seven thousand full-time residents. However, during the Sundance Film Festival or during peak tourist seasons (either summer or winter), Park City's population can easily swell to three times this number. Providing the necessary infrastructure and services to serve these temporary population booms creates a myriad of management challenges.

In an attempt to better serve its citizens and tourists, Park City looked for opportunities to benchmark with similar municipal governments. This search directed Park City to the Colorado Association of Ski Towns (CAST). Park City and the CAST municipalities formed the Resort Community Benchmarking Group (RCBG), which also includes resort communities in Wyoming and Idaho. The goal of the benchmarking project is to "improve existing services, processes, and procedures by learning from our peers and studying their best practices" (Resort Community Benchmarking Group, 2006).

The benchmarking group decided to organize the process into phases. Phase one in the work plan was to examine the participating cities' demographic and fiscal factors on the macro level, including demographics and fiscal health indicators. The second phase of the plan was to create direct comparisons and departmental comparisons. This second phase is more likely to generate best or promising practices.

This resort community project has followed the traditional benchmarking steps exactly (as described in Chapter Four). The process, still in its early stages, has closely followed the first five steps: charter a team, determine purpose and scope, define benchmarking intentions, research potential partners, and choose performance measures. This process is putting Park City and the other participating communities on the right track. Their example also shows that organizations that share a set of circumstances that makes them unique in some way need to pay particular attention to step 4 of the process, researching potential partners. Park City's effort to find apples-to-apples comparisons for its specific situation required this careful methodology.

Utah Benchmarking Project: The First Steps in a Municipal Benchmarking Study

Currently, we have been involved with the Utah Benchmarking Project. This benchmarking venture is similar to the North Carolina Benchmarking Project (discussed earlier in this chapter) in makeup and objective. In 2006, the Utah City Management Association initiated a benchmarking effort, headed by a couple of city managers who were association members. Many of the cities involved had attempted comprehensive benchmarking projects previously but had eventually abandoned them in the face of difficult data collection or lack of staff resources. To encourage greater success, this effort aimed to include additional organizations: the Utah League of Cities and Towns, the University of Utah Center for Public Policy and Administration, the Brigham Young University Marriott School of Management, Utah State University, and Southern Utah University. The first step, charter a team, required the creation of a committee of representatives from each of these organizations. Once the benchmarking team was organized, a number of meetings ensued to determine the scope of the project and a timeline for expected results. The defined purpose of the Utah Benchmarking Project is as follows:

> To provide local governments with a management tool that supports their decision-making process in strategic planning, performance improvement, and accountability. By identifying and establishing standard performance measures, this management tool will facilitate comparisons for any given city against its cluster of cities. Comparisons will provide opportunities for enhanced organizational effectiveness through the identification, communication, and implementation of appropriate best practices [Utah Benchmarking Project, 2007].

Unlike the Resort Community Benchmarking Group, the Utah Benchmarking Project does not emphasize specific benchmarking partners; instead, all Utah municipalities are welcome to join. Currently, around forty municipal governments are participating partners. However, in order to identify more comparable partners, the Utah Benchmarking Project is utilizing a clustering method for the participating cities. This clustering of cities creates potential partners and allows for more direct comparisons. The clustering criterion is based on economic, fiscal, and demographic factors for each city. For example, many of the high-growth cities participating in this study are clustered together for the benchmarking analysis.

The benchmarking team made a considerable effort to define and organize performance measures. This process reflects the similar phases of the resort communities—begin with easy-to-collect demographic and financial indicators; then advance in phase two to more specific data sets. The benchmarking team surveyed the forty participating municipal organizations to determine a priority listing of measurements. To get to this surveying point, the team met regularly (at least once a month) for six months. This methodical process provides a thorough review and builds buy-in from a number of organizations. Yet it also creates a number of challenges. One frequent challenge is getting burned out on the lengthy process before even getting to the phase of best practice identification—something we will address further at the end of the chapter.

One early success of the Utah Benchmarking Project is the survey instrument created by the steering committee. This instrument was administered online to the participating organizations and supplied more specific information for each participating city. This collection of data is laying an important foundation for identifying potential best practices. The benchmarking team followed many of the traditional steps (see Chapter Four): from chartering the team, determining the purpose, and defining the process to researching partners or participants, choosing measurements, collecting internal data, and collecting data from partners. Now the challenge is to sustain the momentum and import practices that close performance gaps.

Benchmarking is a critical management tool for cities to achieve maximum efficiency and effectiveness. Ultimately it is a question of how can we serve our citizens better. Measuring and comparing performance through benchmarking leads to better service delivery, which increases citizen satisfaction.

—Mark Christensen, city manager, Washington Terrace, Utah (personal communication, May 13, 2007)

Stakeholders

As the previous examples illustrate, the individual participants in a benchmarking project play a critical role in seeing the process through to success and the discovery of best practices (as we discussed in greater depth in our previous edition). It is therefore essential to identify and review the roles of specific participants. Key to selecting the right benchmarking partners is identifying stakeholders. The most basic difference between public and private sector benchmarking lies in two groups of individuals who will be involved in virtually any public sector benchmarking project: politicians and the public. Both groups are significant stakeholders and can provide valuable insight into priorities for improvements and service or product performance goals. Also involved in the process, of course, will be appointed leaders and career managers in the area to be benchmarked; they provide the process, history, and policy knowledge. We are not advocating that anyone and everyone should be involved. Rather the benchmarking team should give considerable thought to involving the right people at the right time to ensure success. But who are the right people, and to what end should they be involved? Let's first address the unique public sector benchmarking players: elected officials and citizens.

Elected Officials   Often, elected officials are not leading the charge for a benchmarking study. The role of the elected official should be focused on contributing in two early steps. The first area of involvement occurs during readiness assessment, when the official's ideas and opinions are solicited. Here, the elected official can offer suggestions for priorities, opportunities to improve, and potential private sector methodologies. The second point at which elected officials should be involved is when the team defines the purpose and scope of the benchmarking project. The team should have specific ideas of which processes to benchmark before discussing the topic with officials. Enlisting the support of elected officials from the beginning positions the team to get these officials' assistance during the project, especially if resources are difficult to come by and potential payoffs look good.

Customers or Citizens   Regularly, the role of the public is more indirect. The underlying purpose of many government benchmarking projects, as we previously mentioned, is to enhance either transparency or accountability to the citizens of the benchmarking jurisdiction. However, citizens are not always direct participants in the study. Occasionally, during the chartering of a benchmarking team, a government organization may include a citizen representative to express the collective voice of the public. However, the Oregon example of incorporating the general public in governmental performance measurement, with which we began this chapter, remains more the exception than the norm.

For years the city of Austin, Texas, has closely monitored the performance of each city department. The city's strategy of managing for results has sought to enhance Austin's ability to provide high-quality services at an efficient level. Previously, these departmental performance measures were available to the public through the annual budget document, which meant they were often buried in other material and not easy to access. A few years ago Austin attempted to resolve this problem by creating a publicly accessible performance measures database.

The database provides citizens with an opportunity to review performance measures by department, by department program, or by specific department activity. The data include historical information and current-year budgeted targets as well as current-year actual results (City of Austin, 2007). This has helped to link the city's management strategies to the public.

As in the Oregon example, this performance measurement process is not necessarily benchmarking. However, these publicly accessible measures have been used by other organizations and have led other organizations to benchmark with Austin (just as other states have attempted to replicate the Oregon experience). In sum, there are definite benefits to linking a benchmarking project to the public: performance measures can then reflect citizen priorities, and the overall public perception of government is enhanced.

Earlier in this book we addressed the issue of technology and the effects of the information age on benchmarking. The Austin database is a great example of how the Internet has made performance data more accessible and usable. Organizations that embrace the new online opportunities have been able to reduce some of the previously large hurdles in collecting and sharing performance measurement data. Sharing data is becoming easier and easier due to software packages and technology that allow either the public or the benchmarking partners access to data on line.

In addition to dealing with the inclusion of citizens or other organizations, the benchmarking team must select internal staff to guide the project. First, internal staff are often responsible for creating much of the impetus for the benchmarking project to begin. And second, they are the individuals who offer the hours of manpower to keep it going. Possibly the most significant role is served by those we refer to as *senior leaders*.

Senior Leaders   Department or division heads are likely to be the ones who initiate a benchmarking study. Although this level is a good place to start, it is important that such senior leaders assess the readiness of the other parts of the organization. Benchmarking projects can be difficult for a city if the city manager has not convinced her department heads of the value of the project. For example, collecting the data for specific areas (such as police department information) may be put off by a department when it has no connection to the project, and then the overall work of the senior leaders stalls out. Senior leaders should have a hand in selecting the benchmarking partners and, when possible, participate in the site visits. Finally, senior leaders must be involved in sustaining the desired changes. When the team returns from the site visit and proposes changes, leaders must think strategically and ensure that steps taken in the short term will contribute to long-term success.

In our previous book, we referred to persons who exemplified strong benchmarking leadership as *benchmarking champions;* we continue to use that term here. The benchmarking champion is a senior leader who becomes the strongest advocate for the benchmarking project and thus plays a pivotal role in its success. For example, the leaders driving the Utah Benchmarking Project are the city managers or senior staff positions. Because of her position as a senior leader, the champion is expected to

- Understand the external political factors and seek support for the benchmarking project to ensure its success.
- Ensure that adequate and accurate resources are dedicated to the project.
- Encourage the project coordinator and team members.
- Serve as a liaison between the internal and external benchmarking participants and senior managers.
- Monitor the progress of the project and provide guidance when necessary.
- Interpret results from a strategic and political perspective.
- Design and promote the organizational change necessary to implement the actions designed to bring improvement.

The champion gives strength and continuity to the project. It is the champion, or the group that fills that role, who can make or break a project. Other key team players are the *process owners* and administrative, budget, and audit staff.

Process Owners The people most familiar with the process can provide valuable answers to some of the questions raised in previous chapters: Does the process have improvement potential? Where does it move across departments? What data suggest that the customer is concerned about this process? What attempts have been made to improve the process in the past? Did they succeed or fail? The process owners may contribute the greatest amount of the quantitative information that will be used to gain the support of politicians and to make a final selection when answering many of the essential questions about a project.

Administrative, Budget, and Audit Staff   Public sector budgetary challenges may warrant the involvement of internal fiscal analysts. They can explain how to measure costs or determine how resource intensive processes are invaluable information for selection criteria. A human resource director may be able to offer advice on how to anticipate and deal in advance with the impact of improvement actions. The challenge for many public benchmarking projects is figuring out how to manage these individual team members and stakeholders. Often it requires considerable commitment on the part of the benchmarking champion or leader to keep the team together. Ultimately many benchmarking projects become a discussion of finances at some point. Are we spending more than we should for this service? Is there a more efficient way to budget our money? As the North Carolina Benchmarking Project demonstrates, it makes sense to include the finance experts in this process.

IS THE PUBLIC SECTOR BETTER OFF DUE TO BENCHMARKING?

Has the push for benchmarking really created opportunities for organizations to implement best practices? Or has it just created a culture within the public sector that makes organizations eager to review data just to see how they compare? One danger of the formal benchmarking process is exerting so much effort on the early steps—organizing the team, determining the indicators and measures, collecting and reporting the data—that energy for the project is lost before getting to the discover and implement best practices steps. Knowing a lot of demographic information about neighboring jurisdictions or nationwide associates does not get organizations any closer to improved performance.

From our observations, the evidence stacks up to prove that benchmarking does work in the public sector. However, we also know of cases in which resources were squandered on benchmarking projects that broke down before any change could occur. The public sector is better off when benchmarking leads to implementation of best or promising practices. Benchmarking also makes the public sector better off by creating learning organizations, those in which executives are constantly searching for better and improved ways to deliver performance. They might not find the universal remedy through a benchmarking project, but such a project can at least point a government entity or agency in the direction of progress. We have also found that the public sector is better off using less formal or less traditional benchmarking projects. The less formal approach is addressed more specifically in the next chapter, "Benchmarking in Nonprofits," but we provide an example here of how this method can be used in the public sector. For this case study we turn to a benchmarking effort made by the Salt Lake County Criminal Advisory Council.

CRIMINAL INTAKE IN SALT LAKE COUNTY, UTAH: A SOLUTION-DRIVEN APPROACH IN THE PUBLIC SECTOR

A question that an organization must consider is whether to completely bypass the traditional benchmarking approach. Is a less formal approach a dangerous version of ad hoc benchmarking, or is it a solution-driven approach (as described in Chapter Five)? We believe that both traditional and less formal approaches can be effective.

An example of solution-driven benchmarking at the local government level can be found in Salt Lake County. The story unfolds around Camille Anthony, an attorney who served in the administration of Utah governor Olene Walker. As executive director of Administrative Services, Anthony was responsible for the administration of numerous agencies, including the statewide prison system. In her position she became familiar with state agency performance reports and understood some of the fundamental requirements of the government's data reporting system.

When the administration changed, Anthony, a political appointee, found herself between professional positions. Instead of returning to private, legal practice, she chose to accept a position with the Salt Lake County Criminal Advisory Council.

Working as a staff of one, Camille Anthony quickly realized that the county faced a serious problem. Intake procedures and overcrowding appeared to lead to early release of some prisoners. The county did not receive important inmate information, such as the number of beds available, on a timely basis. This created a situation in which inmates were sometimes transferred to facilities when space was limited and then other inmates were released early to accommodate the incoming people. As the county was potentially in violation of laws, not to mention the situation's potential for inciting public outcry, Anthony felt an urgent need to act. The council had few if any funds to purchase a new information system and was an advisory body only. Neither she nor the council supervised any county staff who could ensure that changes were made.

Anthony had clearly discovered the problem, which is step 1 in the solution-driven benchmarking method. The county was at risk due to the lack of timely and accurate information about inmates. The solution could be defined by a single criterion: the efficient and appropriate processing of prisoner intake and release using timely and accurate data (step 2). Anthony began a search for best practices and accessed professional and personal networks by contacting her former staff and professional associates. With their help she was able to identify several best practices (step 3) for data collection and reporting on prisoner intake and release. Her professional associates also suggested several ways that the existing county system could be modified to ensure proper reporting and decision making.

Anthony was not in a position to simply implement the best practices herself. She served as staff to the Criminal Advisory Council, not to the public safety functions, so she faced the challenging task of convincing the council and the public safety leaders that this problem needed to be solved. (Figure 6.1 illustrates the involvement of some of the stakeholders in this example.) Although it took a few months and many meetings, eventually some of the best practices were incorporated into Salt Lake County's prisoner intake system. Anthony and the council have now moved on to other issues, such as preventing crimes and developing work release programs.

Benchmarking is becoming a key management tool for state and local government leaders. The benefits of comparing performance measures or sharing promising or best practices are noteworthy. Many of the benchmarking efforts of local governments come back to the notion of accountability to citizens. There is significant pressure on state and local leaders to be accountable for their use of tax dollars, use of time, and management of resources. Benchmarking enhances accountability (a focus of Chapter Nine) and also can improve efficiency and customer satisfaction.

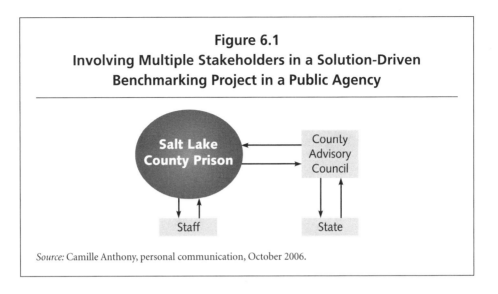

**Figure 6.1
Involving Multiple Stakeholders in a Solution-Driven
Benchmarking Project in a Public Agency**

Source: Camille Anthony, personal communication, October 2006.

Nonprofit organizations have much in common with government agencies, and the pressures to be accountable are similar. Many nonprofits work in tandem with the public sector and often rely on public funding. Additionally, many nonprofits deliver services similar to those the public sector delivers. However, the benchmarking process for the nonprofit sector is slightly different from the process for the public sector. In the next chapter we discuss how the nonprofit sector uses some of the public sector strategies but blends them with a more informal methodology.

SUMMARY

- Benchmarking is becoming a more and more common management tool in the public sector.
- Benchmarking in the public sector is different from benchmarking in other sectors due to the internal and external factors that may influence the process.
- Carefully following many of the traditional eleven steps is important to building strong benchmarking teams and ensuring complete buy-in on a project.

- Best practices can be found and implemented across both state and local governments for all policy areas.
- Careful selection of a benchmarking partner is a particularly important step in the public sector when unique or unusual organizational dynamics are in play.
- Both the traditional and the solution-driven approaches can produce positive results.

Benchmarking in Nonprofits

The nonprofit sector has evolved into a major cultural, economic, and political component of American society (Frumkin & Imber, 2004; O'Neill, 2002; Ott, 2001). Few Americans spend a day without coming into contact with at least one nonprofit, yet many are unaware of the prominence of nonprofits in U.S. communities. The nonprofit sector includes a vast array of organizations ranging from food banks to universities to support groups to social service providers and advocacy organizations. Nonprofits contribute greatly to creating and fostering the quality of life that people enjoy in their neighborhoods. Additionally, nonprofits support the local, state, and national governments through a wide range of contracts for service (Anheier, 2005; Smith & Lipsky, 1993).

Like most organizations, nonprofits face serious challenges in balancing their budgets, raising revenue, improving performance, and meeting patrons' expectations. When contributions and revenues decline, nonprofits must find ways to reduce costs or reduce services. Often reducing services is not a very viable or popular option. Instead, like government and private sector organizations, nonprofit organizations look for ways to streamline and improve. Often this effort requires that managers review other organizations in a search for best practices. Benchmarking offers the nonprofit organization an opportunity to look for best practices systematically and then to adapt those practices to its own functions.

As we have discussed in the previous chapters, a new and effective approach to benchmarking has emerged largely as a result of nonprofit organizations' efforts in this field. Lacking the resources to conduct a traditional benchmarking study, the leaders and executives of nonprofit organizations turned down a different path—one that we refer to as a *solution-driven approach.*

This chapter does not appear in our previous edition of this book. The significant growth and increasing importance of the nonprofit sector have led us to discuss this sector separately in this new edition, and as previously mentioned, we have discovered a unique application of benchmarking in the nonprofit sector. Before we address benchmarking for nonprofits, however, it will be helpful if we review some basic facts about nonprofits and their recent growth.

WHAT IS A NONPROFIT?

Nonprofit organizations, also referred to collectively as the *third sector, voluntary sector, independent sector,* and *nongovernmental organizations* (NGOs), are defined by the U.S. government's Internal Revenue Code (IRC). The IRC lists twenty-eight types of 501(c) organizations, which are exempt from some federal income tax. Most nonprofit organizations are categorized as 501(c)(3) organizations. Common examples of 501(c)(3) organizations are the United Way, American Red Cross, and Salvation Army. A number of political *think tanks* (for example, the Cato Institute and The Heritage Foundation) also operate as 501(c)(3) organizations. This category includes all religious, charitable, and similar organizations. According to the Internal Revenue Service (IRS), in 2001 over half of all nonprofits were 501(c)(3)s. The primary distinction between the nonprofit sector and public and private sectors is the *nondistribution constraint.* Nonprofit organizations provide some service that is forbidden to make a profit for those who control the organization, such as the board of directors or staff. According to more recent research, around 80 percent of the total number of nonprofits nationwide are 501(c)(3) and 501(c)(4) organizations, making up what is commonly referred to as the *independent sector* (Independent Sector, 2007). (Also see Figure 7.1.) More specifically, recent estimates suggest that there are around 1.9 million nonprofit organizations in the United States that are registered with the IRS, of which 1.4 million are considered the independent sector (IRS, 2007; Pollak & Blackwood, 2007). As mentioned, most nonprofit organizations are charitable

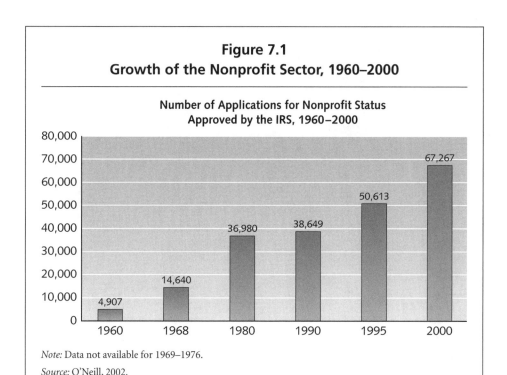

Figure 7.1
Growth of the Nonprofit Sector, 1960–2000

Number of Applications for Nonprofit Status
Approved by the IRS, 1960–2000

Year	Number
1960	4,907
1968	14,640
1980	36,980
1990	38,649
1995	50,613
2000	67,267

Note: Data not available for 1969–1976.

Source: O'Neill, 2002.

nonprofits dedicated to human service delivery programs. There are also a number of nonprofits that focus on education and health care. The nonprofit category also includes some of the traditional civic clubs, such as chambers of commerce and fraternal organizations. However, this is the one area of the nonprofit sector that appears to be in decline (see Table 7.1).

The organizations in the nonprofit sector collectively account for around 5 percent of the U.S. gross domestic product (GDP) and 8.3 percent of all the salaries and wages paid in the United States (Pollak & Blackwood, 2007). Or, to put it another way, the nonprofit sector in the United States generates revenue that exceeds the GDP in all but six foreign countries (O'Neill, 2002). In 2004, public charities reported around $1 trillion in total revenue and expenses (Pollak & Blackwood, 2007).

The organizations in the nonprofit sector are unique and diverse. They range from small community organizations with zero paid staff to very large organizations with billion-dollar budgets. The one consistency is that the magnitude and

Table 7.1

Some Facts About the Nonprofit Sector

	1996		2006		
	NUMBER OF ORGANIZA-TIONS	PERCENTAGE OF ALL ORGANIZATIONS	NUMBER OF ORGANIZA-TIONS	PERCENTAGE OF ALL ORGANIZATIONS	PERCENTAGE OF CHANGE
All nonprofit organizations	1,084,939	100.00%	1,478,194	100.00%	36.20%
501(c)(3) public charities registered with the IRS (including registered congregations)	535,930	49.40%	904,313	61.20%	68.70%
501(c)(3) private foundations	58,774	5.40%	109,852	7.40%	86.90%
Other 501(c) non-profit organizations	490,235	45.20%	464,029	31.40%	−5.30%
Civic leagues, social welfare organiza-tions, and so forth	27,567	11.80%	116,539	7.90%	−8.60%

Fraternal beneficiary societies	102,592	9.50%	84,049	5.70%	– 18.10%
Business leagues, chambers of commerce, and so forth	68,575	6.30%	72,549	4.90%	5.80%
Labor, agricultural, and horticultural organizations	61,729	5.70%	56,460	3.80%	-8.50%
Social and recreational clubs	57,090	5.30%	56,778	3.80%	-0.50%
Posts or organizations of war veterans	30,578	2.80%	35,164	2.40%	15.00%
All other nonprofit organizations	42,104	3.90%	42,490	2.90%	0.90%

Source: Adapted from Urban Institute, National Center for Charitable Statistics, 2007.

influence of the nonprofit sector continues to grow. The growth trends indicate that the nonprofit sector will continue to play an important part in the everyday lives of Americans. However, nonprofit managers still have the burden of leading learning organizations that are able to deliver services in an efficient manner, an achievement that maintains the trust and support of the general public.

PRESSURE TO BENCHMARK

As the number of nonprofits increases so do the resources available to them. For example, the last few decades have presented a number of opportunities for nonprofits to collaborate or contract with government agencies. Today a large number of nonprofit organizations, especially charitable organizations providing social or human services, receive a large portion of their revenue from government grants. In addition, a number of nonprofits are forging strong ties to corporate donors. These additional revenue sources have, overall, strengthened the nonprofit sector; however, they have also introduced a new challenge—public accountability. Meeting this accountability is becoming more and more complex for nonprofits. Historically, nonprofits have been accountable first to their boards and their largest charitable benefactors. Now many nonprofits juggle many levels of accountability stemming from their government contracts, corporate contributions, private donors, boards of directors, and clients receiving the service delivered.

The issue of public accountability has become increasingly critical for nonprofits. In addition, as nonprofits have become more and more prevalent, there has been an increase in scrutiny. Senator Chuck Grassley (R-IA), as chair of the Senate Finance Committee, had a definite agenda to make nonprofit organizations more accountable. Although this effort was directed primarily toward the more political nonprofit organizations, it had effects that rippled throughout the entire nonprofit sector. Many nonprofits came to realize that external benchmarks or performance measures might be imposed on them.

As a result there are mixed responses to benchmarking among nonprofit executive directors. Some embrace a formal process of collecting information and data; however, others see benchmarking as a form of external performance measurement that can threaten organizational autonomy. Regardless, the movement toward benchmarking is sweeping through the nonprofit sector at nearly the same rate as it swept the private sector in the 1980s and the public sector in the 1990s.

At the same time, a closer analysis reveals that benchmarking is not necessarily a new concept to many nonprofit managers. The formal benchmarking process is often met with some resistance, due either to a lack of necessary resources or to a perceived negative performance comparison. Yet nonprofit executives frequently benchmark with other organizations in a process that relies on networks, contacts, and associations. This process is what we have referred to as *solution-driven benchmarking.*

Nonprofit organizations have historically relied on instinct. It is sometimes a type of instinct that leads nonprofit managers to potential board members, potential fundraising opportunities, new programs, and overall new solutions. As Marcia Festen and Marianne Philbin, in *Level Best: How Small and Grassroots Nonprofits Can Tackle Evaluation and Talk Results* (2007), write: "The longer nonprofit leaders are in the field, the more their instincts are honed, and the better able they are to identify a real prospect for a contribution, an alliance that could be mutually beneficial, or a strategy that could offer a solution. Nonprofit staff routinely find themselves sharing their instincts as they identify community needs and brainstorm about what can be done to address them" (p. 1).

We could not agree more with this view. In our experience of working with and interviewing management and staff from nonprofit organizations, we have seen how this honed intuition translates into executive leadership. Strong leadership of this kind is at the heart of solution-driven benchmarking. This way of searching for solutions is not new, but it is now a key aspect of many nonprofits from their inception and is essentially a benchmarking pursuit of best or promising practices. This process of implementing a solution is not the traditional process that is often associated with benchmarking. This search for solutions or best practices relies much more on the leadership of the organization's management or staff.

NONPROFIT LEADERSHIP AND SOLUTION-DRIVEN BENCHMARKING

Solution-driven benchmarking is different from the traditional approach in a number of ways. First, as mentioned previously, the discovery process typically occurs at the executive level. Often managers at this level are already aware of an occurring problem. Their awareness is possibly a result of the honed instinct mentioned earlier but more likely is due to an awareness of performance data. The problem becomes an organizational priority once executive leaders recognize it and begin to search for a solution.

This first step is based more on leadership and less on management; the focus is on the solution—not the problem definition. Managers often do not have time to collect and analyze data. They may analyze if the data are already available, but often they are looking for an urgent solution discovery. So managers are often in a position where the analysis is already done (a good thing), or they skip this step (a risky move). The search for solutions can have positive results because the manager reaches out to partners or others in her or his network to find solutions. (We will discuss this in much more detail later in the chapter.)

In the traditional benchmarking process the problem is typically defined through measures. But when a leader has an intuitive sense that *this* particular problem is urgent, management decides to place more emphasis and resources on finding the solution than on analyzing the problem.

This approach requires that managers streamline the way that they adapt and implement a solution. This approach is similar to traditional benchmarking in that the solution must be adapted. But it differs from traditional benchmarking in that the solution is not adapted by the importing organization in the form of the benchmarking team and other staff. During this streamlined solution-driven approach, one or more managers, not the benchmarking team, set into motion the implementation phase. This process eases the usually difficult traditional step of seeking consent from the proper authority prior to implementation. Ultimately, a manager requires fewer resources for analysis and implementation. She uses her power and authority to find the solution rather than to analyze the problem.

One factor that makes a nonprofit unique during this streamlined solution-driven approach is the role of its board of directors. The role of board members varies significantly across different organizations. Some boards are very hands-off; others want to review and approve even minor details. Obviously, the board can check on management in this process; however, in our experience, most nonprofit boards of directors defer to the expertise of the managers on administrative or service delivery components. Thus the solution-driven process is usually not delayed by the process of seeking board approval and managers have significant flexibility to discover and implement solutions that they find by relying on their own networks.

EXAMPLES OF SOLUTION-DRIVEN BENCHMARKING IN NONPROFITS

As we discussed benchmarking with managers from various nonprofit organizations, we discovered three main factors that contribute to taking a solution-driven approach. First, there is a "we are all in this together" mind-set among many nonprofit organizations. Second, nonprofits typically have a very small number of administrative staff and often rely on volunteers to fill this role. And third, historically, nonprofit organizations have developed highly creative problem-solving processes, which allows them increased administrative flexibility.

The very nature of the nonprofit sector is for the organizations to be highly collaborative. Competitive barriers to communication do not exist in the nonprofit arena as they do in the private sector. Historically, many private organizations have maintained a resistance to sharing information, for fear that it would enable potential competitors. Nonprofits largely have not had to overcome this hurdle. This does not mean there is no competitive spirit in the nonprofit sector; in fact nonprofits often must compete for the same private or corporate donors. Nevertheless organizations in the nonprofit world remain more open and cooperative with each other, and this sentiment extends beyond nonprofit organizations providing the same service. For example, in the early 1990s, many of the arts and culture nonprofits in Utah were struggling financially. These organizations, led by the Utah Symphony, sought a sales tax increase to be dedicated to funding the arts in Salt Lake County, but the initial ballot proposition failed by a three to two margin. The arts community responded by building a coalition with other nonprofit organizations—parks, recreation facilities, and zoological organizations that were also looking for funding from a sales tax increase. Soon a plan was orchestrated to include funding for the arts with funding for these other organizations. In 1997, with this new partnership the tax increase again appeared on the ballot—this time it passed. In 2004, the Zoo, Arts, and Parks (ZAP) tax was reapproved by Salt Lake County voters, with 71 percent in favor. Today, more than one hundred nonprofit organizations in Salt Lake County benefit from the ZAP tax, even with 58 percent of the tax revenue going to nonprofit cultural organizations (Salt Lake County, Utah, 2007). There are numerous examples similar to this one of nonprofit organizations banding together to solve a financial problem.

The Zoo, Arts, and Parks Tax is one of the most widely accepted taxes in the state of Utah. Residents of Salt Lake County overwhelmingly support this tax, because they see the direct benefits of their tax dollars when they go to the park, the zoo, or the symphony. However, this tax would have never been implemented without the broad coalition built among dozens of nonprofits throughout Salt Lake County.

—Jim Bradley, Salt Lake County councilmember
(personal communication, September 17, 2007)

Typically, a nonprofit organization's financial and administrative resources are limited. These limits arise from a couple of factors. First, much of the revenue generated to fund a nonprofit is dedicated specifically to service delivery programs. We could debate whether benchmarking should be considered a service delivery program or not, but the reality is that most funders, donors, and contributors do not view benchmarking activities as service delivery. For example, when someone makes a private contribution to a food bank, he often wants to know that he is paying for food to be delivered—not for sending a food bank staff member to another site to explore whether there is a more efficient way to transport meals. This means that frequently only a small percentage of a nonprofit's funds is not earmarked for certain programs. Second, it can often be difficult for nonprofit organizations, especially the smaller, grassroots organizations, to set aside enough staff time to undertake a traditional benchmarking study.

It is well documented that the nonprofit sector often fills the gap between the public and private sectors. In addition to this role, the nonprofit sector is often viewed as an incubator for solutions. Nonprofits regularly have a considerable flexibility to implement programs. An argument can be made that autonomy and flexibility is the most noteworthy strength of the nonprofit sector. This strength also allows many nonprofit organizations to implement and test best or promising practices with greater ease than other organizations do—they require fewer bureaucratic steps to begin implementation. To restate, each of these factors—collaborative nature, limited resources, and creative problem-solving practice—leads to the frequent use of solution-driven benchmarking in the nonprofit sector.

Discovery Gateway, Salt Lake City, Utah

When the leaders and staff of the Utah Children's Museum, now named Discovery Gateway, began plans to expand to a new and larger facility, one of their first actions was to ask, "Who has experienced this move before?" They discovered a piece of their answer from the Children's Museum of Pittsburgh. The Children's Museum of Pittsburgh had similarly transitioned from a smaller facility to a much larger building and operation. After many visits from Utah staff to the Pittsburgh museum (along with visits to a number of other children's museums) and after sharing data and analysis, the Discovery Gateway leaders and staff were better prepared to begin the transition. This sharing of ideas did not provide every answer, but it definitely provided some valuable direction for program creation and implementation, exhibit design, administrative direction, and overall management.

The mission of Discovery Gateway is "To inspire children of all ages to imagine, discover, and connect with their world to make a difference" (Discovery Gateway, 2007). In 1978, a group of dedicated parents, educators, and community leaders had joined together to create the Children's Museum of Utah. For years the children's museum fulfilled its mission by providing opportunities for kids of all ages to learn, create, and explore. However, in 2003, thanks in part to funding from Salt Lake County and a partnership with the Junior Achievement of Utah, the Utah Children's Museum began the transition to a more comprehensive world-class hands-on learning center. In 2006, the Utah Children's Museum changed its name to Discovery Gateway, and in the same year, it moved to a new seventy-four-thousand-square-foot facility. This move has proven to be extremely successful. Before they ventured the move, the Utah Children's Museum leaders and staff used benchmarking to reveal many promising practices that have now been successfully implemented.

A $32 million investment for a new facility created many extraordinary opportunities for Discovery Gateway. However, moving from a facility of fifteen thousand square feet to a location at least four times larger also presented some unique challenges. The museum needed to reevaluate and expand virtually all of its programs and services. Yet before it could implement programs, it needed to adopt a design for the new facility also.

When it came time to begin the design, Joanna Fisher, Discovery Gateway director of exhibits, had a clear idea of what she expected. In her words, she wanted an exhibit that demonstrated "wow." This wow component was clearly distinguishable for Fisher—seven photos of exhibits that demonstrated the wow factor were placed prominently on her refrigerator at home. These photos were taken during a series of site visits to other nonprofit children museums. Fisher and other Discovery Gateway staff visited museums across the country in Massachusetts, New York, Florida, Louisiana, California, Indiana, Minnesota, and Oregon. Fisher compiled best or promising practices from the exhibits in each of these comparable museums, mostly through one-on-one communication with her counterpart staff members. This research provided a clear picture of not only her design vision but also the necessary lighting and scale. According to exhibit designer Mindy Lehrman Cameron, the detailed expectations really improved the design process. As the *Deseret Morning News* reported, "Lehrman Cameron says she was happy that Fisher had such specific goals. The more specific a client can be, she says, the more the designer can stretch and play with the ideas and make them even better" (Whitney, 2006).

In addition to improving the exhibit design, Discovery Gateway also sought best practices from other nonprofit children's museums for staff, management, and program creation. For example, Discovery Gateway implemented a new floor-staffing policy that emphasized more guest interaction with staff—a policy that was currently being used by both the Children's Museum of Pittsburgh and the Ontario Science Center in Toronto.

Through this process of research and evaluation, Discovery Gateway created benchmarks for performance. The Children's Museum of Pittsburgh became a key benchmarking partner due to its comparable size and recent similar experience. Even the opening day attendance was measured against Pittsburgh's benchmark. On the opening day of Discovery Gateway in September 2006, attendance exceeded expectations by 70 percent, with 1,700 children and other family members visiting the museum. "The new Children's Museum of Pittsburgh had just over 1,000 visitors on their opening day," said D. D. Hilke, president and CEO of Discovery Gateway. "We are gratified by this show of community interest and support" (Discovery Gateway, 2006).

The benchmarking process that incorporated some traditional steps with a collaborative solution-driven approach led to great success for Discovery Gateway.

Discovery Gateway served 120,000 visitors in its first four months; this total is 20,000 more people than the organization previously served on average for an entire year.

Discovery Gateway's Solution-Driven Benchmarking Steps

- *Discover the problem.* Discovery Gateway identified the potential challenges created by the opportunity to move to a new, larger facility.

- *Establish criteria for solutions.* Discovery Gateway prioritized planning in preparation for the move and established goals to achieve a smooth transition.

- *Search for promising practices.* Discovery Gateway identified organizations that could potentially provide best or promising practices. Numerous site visits and in some cases in-depth collaboration helped leaders and staff identify practices for Discovery Gateway to implement.

Utah Food Bank Services

In 2006, Utah Food Bank Services (UFBS) distributed over eighteen million pounds of food across the state of Utah. However, this 501(c)(3) nonprofit is more than just a food bank. UFBS also provides significant services to senior citizens, low-income children, and people with disabilities. Services such as providing hot meals for low-income kids after school or assisting senior citizens with small home repairs affect thousands of lives every day. To deliver such services, UFBS relies heavily on volunteer assistance. In 2006, it used volunteers every day of the year, receiving 206,000 volunteer hours, or the equivalent of the work of ninety-nine full-time employees, a value of $3.5 million (Utah Food Bank, 2006).

UFBS tracks data on everything. Efficiency is a foremost responsibility of a food bank, especially with perishable food items needing to be stored and transported. If transportation is delayed, food could be wasted and valuable resources lost. UFBS, particularly in its food bank service, has benefited from both formal and informal benchmarking pursuits. An association with the national organization America's Second Harvest (which we discuss in more depth later in the chapter) has introduced UFBS to that organization's annual network activity report, which provides detailed organizational data for food banks across the country. From this report and with some initiative from its executive director Jim Pugh, UFBS has identified helpful benchmark partners. UFBS attempts to find food bank organizations that are similar in size in terms of warehouse capacity and distribution, and it has identified such organizations in San Antonio, Denver, and Seattle, for example. However, UFBS also benchmarks with food banks that share the unique distribution challenge of servicing an entire state, as is the case for some organizations in Idaho, Montana, and Wyoming. UFBS frequently schedules time for site visits with both these types of organizations and often collaborates with them, either reviewing existing programs or discussing potential ideas.

Essentially, the role of benchmarking for UFBS is to create a heightened degree of accountability to private and corporate donors and to thousands of volunteers. One of the most frequent questions potential contributors ask of the UFBS development director is "How much food will this amount buy." As they do with many other nonprofits, people contributing to this food bank want to ensure that their contributions are going directly to service delivery. This places administrative pressure on the staff to reduce any possible inefficiency. The UFBS Kids Cafe is a good example of this scenario.

Kids Cafe is a national program that started in Savannah, Georgia. UFBS's Kids Cafe program provides weeknight dinner meals to low-income youths along with nutritional education to help children and their families lead healthier lives. Currently, a community kitchen run by UFBS provides between 700 and 1,000 after-school meals daily to low-income children throughout Utah (primarily in Salt Lake County). Students from UFBS's Community Kitchen program, a culinary training program for low-income individuals, help prepare these meals. This effort requires coordination with sixteen café sites, including schools, community centers, and Boys and Girls Clubs. When UFBS began its Kids Cafe program, it created specific internal performance measures to direct program operations. These measures include the exact nutritional value of each type of meal, the percentage of waste, the staff preparation and serving time required, and the exact cost per meal for each child served. These measures became very useful when UFBS applied for grants or funding to help support the Kids Cafe. For example, the USDA Child & Adult Care Food Program (CACFP) provides federal reimbursement funding for the Kids Cafe program through the Utah Department of Education. CACFP works to assure a healthy, well-balanced variety of nourishing foods for children and adults in day care away from home. The program offers reimbursement for meal service expenses and other aid to eligible child care centers, family and group day care homes, adult day care centers, and outside-school-hours care programs which serve meals to children and adults (Utah State Office of Education, 2007). CACFP funding requires very specific federal nutrition standards to be met with each meal. Snacks and meals provided for children must include a combination of basic nutrition components including choices of milk, juice, grain, fruits and vegetables, and/or meat. There are also precise serving size standards. UFBS was in a good position to demonstrate compliance with the requirements of the grant because its internal performance measurements provided the data that it needed to know in order to serve meals below the required cost that were also at the necessary nutrition level. Additionally, the food bank could provide data collected over time to verify not only that it could comply with the requirements but that it was already operating to provide these after-school meals consistently at an efficient rate. We address in later chapters the importance of monitoring implemented practices, but here UFBS illustrates the success a nonprofit organization can have through establishing internal performance monitoring practices.

Utah Food Bank Services Solution-Driven Benchmarking Steps

- *Search for promising practices.* UFBS relies on a regional network and participation in America's Second Harvest (national association) to determine benchmarking partners.

- *Implement promising practices.* UFBS has implemented Kids Cafe as a new program service in Utah.

- *Monitor progress.* UFBS closely monitors the number of Kids Cafe meals served, average child participation, days on which sites serve food, and several other aspects of the sites and shares these performance measures monthly with America's Second Harvest.

eNONPROFIT BENCHMARKS STUDY

In the Introduction to this book we stressed the need to reevaluate benchmarking practices in light of technological advances. In this section we review the eNonprofit Benchmarks Study, conducted in 2006 under the direction of M+R Strategic Services and the Advocacy Institute. The study closely evaluated data and statistics from three distinct sources. First, fifteen nonprofit organizations (six environmental organizations, six civil or legal rights organizations, and three international aid organizations) were made study partners. Second, aggregate data from three major providers of online communication (Convio, GetActive Software, and Kintera) were collected. And lastly, an online survey of the broader nonprofit community was conducted (with eighty-five nonprofits responding). The study uncovered eight recommended best practices, and we will review a few here. (For the full report see M+R Strategic Services & Advocacy Institute, 2006.)

With the arrival of the dot-com era, the role of e-mail has become increasingly important across all organizations. E-mail has become the preferred mode of communication in many organizations, and it is especially important to the development or fundraising function in many nonprofits. E-mail is also frequently used to convey advocacy messages. In their study, M+R Strategic Services and the Advocacy Institute evaluated a number of interesting e-mail dynamics, including message length, message grade level, day sent (day of the week), and e-mail list size. The most significant factor appeared to be e-mail list size. Data from the fifteen nonprofit study partners showed that their e-mail list sizes ranged from 10,000 to 600,000 recipients. One of the best practices discovered by this study is that organizations with larger e-mail lists were better able to achieve online fundraising and advocacy success. Growing an e-mail list is one key way to improve results.

Along with this discovery, the study highlighted the need for organizations to churn, or revise, their e-mail lists. According to this research, 28 percent of all e-mail subscribers can become unreachable within twelve months of a list's creation. Therefore another best practice recommended is that nonprofit organizations anticipate performing frequent list reviews or establish some criteria for churning list subscribers.

Another interesting finding from this benchmarking research concerns the best day of the week for sending advocacy messages. According to the study authors, advocacy messages sent on Thursdays and Fridays are opened slightly more often than e-mails sent out during the week. These data contradict the widely held notion that e-mails are most effective if sent out earlier in the week. This is definitely a best practice that could easily be implemented and tested in individual nonprofit and public organizations.

The Internet has created many new opportunities for nonprofit managers. Fundraising, for example, has been significantly affected by the Internet. Not only is online fundraising an option for most nonprofits but the ability to link appropriate stories to opportunities to give is greatly increased by the Internet.

For example, in the aftermath of Hurricane Katrina a number of articles about the resulting crisis included direct links to the Red Cross or other reputable charity organizations. This practice facilitates fundraising efforts. This eNonprofit Benchmarking Study is a great example of nonprofit organizations serving different service delivery areas collaborating together to search for best or promising practices.

SELECTING POTENTIAL BENCHMARKING PARTNERS

One of the initial steps for either the traditional or the solution-driven benchmarking process is selecting potential benchmarking partners. Sometimes this selection process employs extensive data collection and analysis, but often people look to those whom they already trust.

Sometimes we might take the time to read a professional review of a movie or watch Roger Ebert[,] an expert film critic. Yet often we choose to attend a movie based on having a friend recommend it—many times we chose best practices the same way. A friend recommended it.

—Don Gomes, executive director,
Utah Nonprofits Association
(personal communication July 26, 2007)

The number of individuals and organizations that a person trusts depends on a variety of factors. First, many of these relationships depend on personal contacts or friendships between executives. However, trust can also often be built up among organizations that belong to the same national association or similar organization. For example, America's Second Harvest is a national food bank network based in Chicago. More than two hundred food banks from every state in America are members of this network. The mission of America's Second Harvest is to "feed America's hungry through a nationwide network of member food banks and engage our country in the fight to end hunger" (America's Second

Harvest, 2007). America's Second Harvest gets food and financial donations from across the country, resources that it distributes to food banks. In 2006, it distributed two billion pounds of food. America's Second Harvest helps facilitate benchmarking by playing two key roles. First, each year, the America's Second Harvest Network collects data from member food banks on their operations and publishes them in a network activity report (NAR) that presents information in such report categories as operational statistics, financial reports, performance indicators, and member profiles. In total, America's Second Harvest offers fifty different reports, covering every aspect of member food bank operations. This collection of data assists food banks across the nation, helping them to determine indicators for performance measurement and to select benchmark partners based on member profiles.

In addition this collection of data also provides a forum through which organizations can network together to build relationships. It is through years of association in these national networks that administrators and executives began to build their trust circles, and often it is through these trusted contacts that best practices are found. As part of this networking, America's Second Harvest manages an e-mail list serve. This list serve serves as a type of electronic or Internet forum, allowing an organization to send out a question and receive responses from numerous other organizations in minutes or days. Although this activity does not produce a best practice initially, it does generate momentum and enables an organization to target a partner to seek more information. America's Second Harvest is an example of a national association bringing regional and state organizations together; however, it is not unique. Virtually every type of nonprofit organization participates in a larger national association, and many of these associations provide benefits similar to the ones outlined here.

THINKING AHEAD

As mentioned throughout the book and in this chapter, the dot-com era has in many ways changed people's communication habits, including the methods they use to seek best practices and the ease with which they can do these searches. When people see a potential problem or are seeking a new idea, they frequently turn first to Google and search a few keywords; next they e-mail some of their friends or they send out an e-mail on a list serve that they belong to. All these methods begin the gold rush process of solution-driven benchmarking.

As the dot-com era transitions into what is commonly referred to as Web 2.0, online collaboration is becoming more and more common. Web 2.0 refers to Web-based social networks, which in recent years have become incredibly popular. These networks might feature blogs or wikis or a Facebook for college students. In addition, podcasts and other video streaming enhance people's ability to provide and access information via the Internet. All of this really boils down to a sharing of ideas and information. Obviously, much of this information does not result in best practices—it does, however, increase the ease with which people can search for practices. The Internet has created a world without borders, and the twenty-first century has advanced everyone's ability to navigate this world through a click of the mouse on a laptop in his or her home. In our opinion the ease of sharing information in the twenty-first century has increased the use of the solution-driven benchmarking methodology.

SUMMARY

- The nonprofit sector has grown into a major component of service delivery in the United States, often partnering with the private or public sector.

- Performance measurements are becoming increasingly significant to nonprofits, due to both external and internal pressures.

- The nonprofit sector is by nature highly collaborative, which has fed a solution-driven benchmarking strategy for many organizations.

- Limited resources, either financial or administrative, have also increased the need for a solution-driven approach.

- Many nonprofits have the flexibility and autonomy to implement the best practices that they discover through solution-driven methods; often their implementation process is free of some of the bureaucratic challenges facing the public sector.

Benchmarking in the International Community

Benchmarking has definitely become an international phenomenon. You may be surprised to learn how Scotland compared itself to Costa Rica, or how best practices for financial management and improving footpaths took form in Niger and Bangalore, respectively. Similarly, several Pacific island governments have benchmarked with each other on financial performance despite their geographical distance from each other. Australian local governments have been successfully benchmarking for almost fifteen years, and the mass-transit organizations in Mexico City, New York City, Paris, London, and Moscow (and other cities) have been benchmarking for about eleven years.

GENERAL CHARACTERISTICS OF INTERNATIONAL BENCHMARKING

Two general observations can be made about the international community and benchmarking before we move on to the examples.

The Methodology Is Stable

Although the international community has applied benchmarking to a wide variety of problems and processes, it has not significantly modified the traditional method to do so. Virtually all of the international cases presented in this chapter have applied most of the steps in the traditional benchmarking method.

Several countries initially launched their benchmarking teams with training, and others used consultants to guide the benchmarking process. The consistency in their use of the traditional approach and its individual steps, once again drives home the reliability and validity of this method for searching for best practices. There is also a spark of evidence that the solution-driven benchmarking method exists in the international community as well. It is only a matter of time before it too becomes widely adopted as a tool for searching for promising practices.

Developing Countries Are Using It

With illustrations from Niger, Bangalore, and countries in the Pacific region, we discuss how these developing regions are using benchmarking as they develop their infrastructures, economies, and financial management processes. In all of these cases the developing countries and benchmarking projects were encouraged and supported by other nations or organizations. The Asian Development Bank (ADB), the World Bank, and the U.S. Department of Interior's Office of Insular Affairs (OIA) provided training and funding for aspects of these benchmarking projects. The use of benchmarking techniques in developing countries suggests two points. First, benchmarking is a tool that can be easily understood, taught, and applied at a fundamental level. Second, more advanced nations appear to use benchmarking to help mentor less developed nations. It should not be too surprising, given the success enjoyed in westernized countries, that the more developed nations want to share benchmarking with the less developed ones.

EXAMPLES OF INTERNATIONAL BENCHMARKING
Pacific Region

In 1991, the Graduate School, USDA, through an interagency agreement with the OIA, established the Pacific Islands Training Initiative (PITI) and the Virgin Islands Training Initiative (VITI). One of the PITI/VITI goals was to build the knowledge and skills of the public sector employees on Guam, American Samoa, the Republic of Palau, the Commonwealth of the Northern Mariana Islands, the Federated States of Micronesia, the Republic of the Marshall Islands, and the U.S. Virgin Islands. A few years into these programs a considerable amount of training and capacity building had been accomplished. Leaders in the PITI and VITI programs recognized the need to advance these skills one step further and asked that OIA support a series of events to assist the insular governments, through professional networks and opportunities, to compare operational performance. With financial and other support from OIA, PITI/VITI successfully created a variety of benchmarking opportunities.

Association of Pacific Islands Public Auditors   A primary tenet of democracy is transparency and accountability. Each island government had established a government-wide, independent audit office to provide oversight of the various executive branch agencies. The Association of Pacific Islands Public Auditors (APIPA) was created to provide an annual forum to auditors in these governments for training and comparing performance (2003). Since APIPA's inception over eighteen years ago, these annual conferences have been held, and members have established a peer review process.

What does this have to do with benchmarking? It set the stage for two things: First, auditors in the Pacific island governments have shared best practices. Initially, the audit offices conducted only financial audits. As Guam and the Commonwealth of the Northern Mariana Islands (CNMI) launched into program audits, the other islands followed their lead and incorporated Guam's and CNMI's best practices in doing so. Second, the Pacific island auditors became leaders in promoting comparisons among the governments. As we discuss further in Chapter Ten, auditors can promote the concepts of best practices and benchmarking but are somewhat limited in their ability to conduct actual benchmarking studies. Through APIPA's efforts, member governments have been nudged into the world of performance assessment and comparisons.

The Pacific island governments have made significant performance improvements through benchmarking, the Performeter, and identification of best practices.

Stephen Latimer, program director,
Pacific Island Training Initiatives
(personal communication, May 2007)

Island Government Finance Officers Association   In Chapter Five, "The Solution-Driven Benchmarking Method," you were introduced to Lourdes Perez, director of Guam's Department of Administration from 2003 to 2007 and president of the Island Government Finance Officers Association (IGFOA). Another organization born from the work of OIA and the PITI/VITI leaders, IGFOA promoted a benchmarking tool it calls the *Performeter*. The Performeter displays financial data, such as revenues and expenditures, from these island nations and is used by OIA and the insular governments to track key financial ratios over time. Unfortunately, it has not yet been used by legislators or chief executives to make financial decisions. It has, however, served as a framework for IGFOA members to identify and discuss best practices.

Meeting twice a year, the IGFOA members incorporate steps of the solution-driven method into their meetings. For example, in 2003 they identified late financial statements as a key problem (step 1: discover the problem). Their measure for success was simple—issue financial statements on time (step 2: establish criteria for solutions). They discussed the various causes of the late statements and found a variety of opportunities for island governments to improve. Promising practices included setting deadlines for contributing agencies and preparing some reports well in advance of the current timeline (step 4: implement promising practices). Since then all but one of the governments have issued their financial statements on time. More important, IGFOA members are following this same process to address audit exceptions found on their financial statements. The Republic of Palau was the first to have a "clean audit," partly owing to the promising practices found through IGFOA. The forethought and consistent support of OIA and the PITI/VITI leaders has reaped a considerable harvest through APIPA and IGFOA.

VisitScotland

VisitScotland, the national tourist board of Scotland, has been involved with a particularly comprehensive international benchmarking effort (VisitScotland .com, 2007). In 2002, a series of benchmarking studies led by John Lennon, director of the Moffat Centre for Travel and Tourism Business Development at Glasgow Caledonian University, was conducted for VisitScotland. A major purpose of these studies was to find and analyze best practices related to the tourism industry in seven countries and one province: Scotland, Austria, New Zealand, Ireland, Costa Rica, South Africa, Germany, and British Columbia.

The benchmarking method closely tracked the traditional approach that we described in Chapter Four. One of the first steps was to form the research team and determine the project's scope. The eight regions were compared on a variety of numbers, such as level of growth, visitors per square kilometer, and tourist expenditure per region. After initial research, the best practices were developed through site visits to each region. Ultimately, dozens of best practices were assembled into eight categories.

Main lessons from the statistical analysis. The statistical analysis indicated that Scotland was lagging behind British Columbia, Ireland, and New Zealand in its ability to attract high-spending tourists. Also, Scotland did not perform as well as the other regions as a holiday destination for its own residents. Rather than uncovering best practices, the statistical analysis helped VisitScotland's benchmarking team to understand Scotland's performance relative to others and to better define areas in need of best practices.

Role of the central government. The Irish government has a twenty-year history of closely tying its strategic priorities to the tourism industry and has funded those priorities accordingly. Scotland rarely links its strategies to costs and sources of funding; thus, VisitScotland considered the Irish government's approach to strategic priorities and funding a best practice.

Role of national tourism. All the regions in the study were found to have national or provincial tourism organizations and central funding. Germany, New Zealand, and South Africa take an initial step of also participating in organized international activities. For example, South Africa partners with neighboring countries and islands in marketing schemes to attract tourists to the entire area. VisitScotland deems the link between the national tourism organization and cooperative international activities a best practice.

Operational structures. The benchmarking studies revealed several inefficient or duplicative operational structures in many of the regions, especially in South Africa and Germany. The best practices were limited in this category, but nonetheless a few emerged. For example, Costa Rica's national tourism office was organized to have direct access to that country's president. British Columbia, whose tourism industry is well developed, allows the private sector to dominate many of the strategies and activities and organizes its tourism office accordingly.

Role of strategic planning and of funding the tourism industry. The role of the central government in tourism in Ireland is closely linked to how the government integrates the strategic planning process and what funds are available. The way Ireland links the two was repeatedly seen as a model and best practice. Additionally, New Zealand's proposed strategic planning process for tourism included a fifty-fifty partnership with the private sector—also seen as a promising practice.

Public-private partnerships. Best practices clearly emerged around the roles played by the private sector in all the partner regions in the benchmarking study. Scotland's private sector had played a minor role in developing the tourism industry compared to the private sector role in the partner regions. Private sector organizations in Costa Rica, New Zealand, and British Columbia greatly influenced each region's direction and growth. New Zealand was striving to make its private sector influence even stronger.

Marketing. This category yielded the highest number of best practices for VisitScotland to consider. Ireland's tourism industry had changed its marketing focus from volume to quality and long-term yield. Several countries, such as Costa Rica and Germany, established seminars or themes to promote tourism. These seminars and themes ensured that a consistent message would be delivered to industry businesses, tourists, and the public at large. South Africa used ambassadors to market and promote its tourism industry.

Services for the industry and information for the visitors. Germany, South Africa, and British Columbia provided financial assistance for developing small to medium-sized businesses in tourism. A New Zealand radio station provided a mechanism for distributing information that was not used by others. Volunteers were used in information centers in New Zealand and British Columbia—VisitScotland had not used volunteers in this capacity.

Results of the VisitScotland benchmarking studies provided Scotland with a great opportunity to boost its tourism industry. To date, VisitScotland has incorporated many of these practices. (To learn more visit its Web site at www.visitscotland.com.)

Australia

In Australia, the Local Government Ministers' Conference (LGMC) has conducted numerous multifaceted benchmarking studies throughout the country, encompassing many of the services common to Australian local governments. In 1994, the LGMC launched a seminal initiative via a national steering committee that guided comparisons of seven different government services. In this landmark project, the LGMC closely followed the traditional benchmarking method as it analyzed fleet maintenance, home care services, library services, payroll production, and rates notification and collection. LGMC developed flowcharts, costs, and best practices for each category in selected cities and local government areas throughout the country. It identified a variety of promising practices from the study. Perhaps most important were the lessons learned for benchmarking. Robert Camp (1998) reports that as a result of side benefits such as improved understanding and communication among the benchmarking team members, many subsequent benchmarking projects ensued.

In January 2006, the South Australian LGMC funded a benchmarking study of management practices among its member governments (Williams, 1998). The project carefully defined benchmarking and best practices, administered and analyzed surveys, and reported award-winning projects that exemplify best practices. Interestingly, the study reported that city managers made a distinction between formal academic benchmarking and continuous improvement—the latter included measurements; comparison of practices, methods, and processes; and an attempt to improve. Nonetheless, results of the study identified four cities and local government areas with promising practices. Two, Alexandrina and Playford, have been selected to illustrate the practices.

In 2001, the Alexandrina Council created its Best Practice in Customer Service project. The goal was to find ways to offer council (that is, government) services at one location and time, six days per week. The council and business community created a vision for the one-stop center, which would mesh with the existing buildings and ambiance. The council, local businesses, and citizens created a logo and a marketing strategy for the new services. Alexandrina's effort was recognized by an Australian Service Excellence Award given by the Customer Service Institute of Australia.

In 2003, the city of Playford created a Peer Student Mentoring Scheme that partnered students from the University of South Australia with local high school students on projects to build robots using leading-edge technology and programming skills. The project reduced truancy, increased high school retention rates, and opened doors to better employment opportunities for the participants. Playford's achievement was recognized in 2003 by a Leading Practice Award for Management Improvement from the National Office of Local Government.

Niger

Weaknesses in financial management across the World Bank's community driven development (CDD) efforts in the Africa region, especially in Niger, prompted the World Bank to commission a benchmarking study (Neighbor, 2001). The study identified and promoted best practices to strengthen financial management capacity and internal accountability in community development projects. The method that World Bank used more closely resembled solution-driven benchmarking than it did traditional benchmarking because it was dependent primarily on the work of one individual who networked across organizations and researched professional guidelines to develop best practices. The best practices discovered by this project may appear to some to be common and expected practices for Western governments. However, these best practices are as important to developing countries, such as Niger, as any best practice is to a Western country. The Niger communities recommended considering over forty best practices.

One of these promising practices was to appoint an itinerant internal auditor to reinforce community involvement and to facilitate financial management capacity through training and regular visits. Another promising practice discovered during the study was for Niger to create an association of chartered accountants. Once begun, this association officially recognized Niger's growing professional accounting and auditing organizations and discouraged unqualified accounting practitioners. Along with several procurement-related practices, the association also established regional bank accounts, which reduced the amount of cash communities were keeping on hand—two best practices related to handling funds. Several promising practices addressed the need for training and procedure manuals. The Niger benchmarking project had the added benefit of being applicable to other countries' portfolios, thereby creating a list of best practices for World Bank CDDs.

CoMET

The Community of Metros (CoMET; 2007), a consortium of metropolitan railways, was founded in 1994 with the original member cities of Hong Kong, New York, London, Paris, and Berlin. These cities had completed some railway benchmarking studies prior to CoMET, but many of their intended studies had failed. CoMET was founded, in part, to sustain benchmarking studies across cities so that they yielded tangible results. Since CoMET's inception other metro areas—such as

Madrid, São Paolo, and Shanghai—have joined CoMET. (A sister organization, Nova, was formed by medium-sized metro areas for similar reasons.) Each year, CoMET conducts a variety of studies on issues ranging from operations to strategies to policies. The benchmarking group is owned and managed by the participants; those cities that have integrated the benchmarking projects into their internal railway systems have been the most successful.

Performance measures play a key role in evaluating when and where to focus improvement efforts. The mix of measures includes the following ratios:

- Total fatalities to total passenger journeys (km)
- Revenue per car per kilometer/total staff and contractor hours
- Fare revenue to passenger journey (km)
- On-time passenger journeys to total passenger journeys
- Total commercial revenue to operating cost
- Total operating cost per car (km)

One study benchmarked CoMET fare policies against those of other European and American railway systems. CoMET members handily covered operating costs through fare revenue but had lost sight of the overall objectives associated with providing public transportation. The European and American partners considered social and political objectives as well as the need to cover operating expenses when determining fares. As a result, some CoMET members integrated social and political issues into discussions of fare strategies with their governing boards and the public.

Benchmarking studies have yielded several best practices. For example, one CoMET member reorganized drivers' shifts, which resulted in a 10 percent increase in productivity. Better station management in Hong Kong led to a 12 percent reduction in station staff (although some would argue that staff reductions should not be a result of benchmarking studies). Finally, a higher penalty on fare evasion was imposed by one metro after benchmarking with others.

CoMET benchmarking studies clearly illustrate the long-term benefits of benchmarking within an industry. It is interesting to note that the CoMET members conducted benchmarking studies individually but that they achieved real breakthrough performances when they established *common* measures and organized regular benchmarking studies. Working together toward continuous improvement is a good investment.

Bangalore

Bangalore is India's technology corridor and one of Asia's fastest growing metropolises. Unfortunately, millions of its citizens live in poor urban slums where literacy rates are quite low, especially for females. The local government institutions primarily responsible for government services in the Bangalore urban agglomeration are the town councils and the Bangalore Mahanagara Palike (BMP). Through a cooperative effort among Bangalore municipalities and with funding through the Asian Development Bank, several benchmarking initiatives have been successfully completed. The first step was to train BMP officials in how to identify service priorities, how to map processes, how to compare and learn from others, and how to implement solutions. A variety of services were selected for benchmarking.

An interesting example is the result achieved by benchmarking footpaths. The existing footpaths were in a deplorable and hazardous condition. Initial measures indicated that 80 percent of footpath users were urban poor and that users' level of satisfaction was 9 percent. In many instances women and children avoided the footpaths due to safety hazards, only to walk along the busy roadways. The BMP funded best practice improvements, which resulted in an increase of satisfaction to 63 percent. Moreover, 93 percent of the people on foot now use the upgraded footpaths instead of the streets.

Bangalore also benchmarked ways to train adolescent girls and women to improve their employment opportunities. Each year, BMP now trains about four thousand females in tailoring. The successful candidates receive certificates that make them professionally and commercially acceptable to the market. More important, each successful candidate receives a sewing machine to help her start working. More than 90 percent of the trained women are now employed either full or part time.

These Bangalore examples demonstrate that even the poorest communities can capitalize on the experiences of others through benchmarking for best practices. Rather than have organizations such as the Asian Development Bank or the United Nations simply disperse answers, these benchmarking projects build capacity by training officials to use benchmarking tools and by allowing citizens to provide input and feedback to the projects. Ultimately, this builds pride in the local communities and confidence in the citizens who participate.

LESSONS LEARNED

Several themes emerge from the international cases that should be acknowledged as lessons learned. In virtually all of the cases, some training or coaching in the benchmarking method was provided to the team. This suggests that the transfer of knowledge and skills in benchmarking methods is important to its continued use and proper application.

Second, in most of the cases, the benchmarking process compares performance among processes or practices held in common—apples to apples. Breakthrough performance can occur without having to go to great lengths to make unusual comparisons. CoMET members, for example, regularly compare transit practices. Also, promising practices can be discovered through broad comparisons as well as in-depth process comparisons. VisitScotland discovered numerous best practices related to strategic planning and the relationship of national tourism to surrounding international communities, whereas teams in Niger and Bangalore delved into specific processes, such as how to handle cash and how to improve walking paths.

Finally, the solution-driven method holds promise for the international community. This method is a less documented benchmarking process, and so it is unclear whether the professional contacts and associations it requires are available and whether they will support its streamlined approach. However, the examples we found in the Pacific region suggest that success with this method in international settings is very possible.

SUMMARY

- Numerous examples of benchmarking can be found throughout the world.
- In many cases, organizations are benchmarking internationally.
- The traditional benchmarking method is the most commonly used method of international benchmarking.
- Training and coaching play an important role in transferring knowledge of benchmarking and skill in using the methodology.
- Broad comparisons across a single industry or among organizations with much in common as well as specific process comparisons can yield promising practices and performance improvement.

- The solution-driven benchmarking method is relatively unknown in the international community but could become widespread where professional and personal networks and associations are available.

Use Worksheet 8.1, in the Resources, to evaluate your own organization's readiness for international benchmarking.

PART FOUR Benchmarking and Accountability

Most individuals and organizations would be very happy if they never had to report to anyone about performance, problems, inefficiencies, or spending. But reality is quite different and for good reasons. As individuals, we all balance our own bank accounts, manage our credit, enjoy many public sector products and services, and expect value for our dollar. As citizens in our nation, we hold individuals and organizations accountable for their actions through our laws and we hold our government accountable through its many checks and balances. When left unchecked, governments and nonprofit organizations can become inefficient, ineffective, and downright irresponsible.

In Chapter Nine, "Benchmarking for Improving Accountability," we discuss evidence that accountability has come to the forefront of people's attention and is here to stay. We also introduce several ways benchmarking can play a positive and effective role in ensuring that resources are directed to the right places and used in the most efficient and effective manner. We argue that public and nonprofit leaders and managers can use benchmarking to enhance accountability.

Chapter Ten, "Benchmarking and Performing an Audit," suggests that a discussion about accountability is not complete without including the audit world. The auditor's life is dedicated to holding people and organizations accountable.

Can auditors integrate benchmarking into audit methodologies? Yes, but auditors are not likely to use benchmarking in the same manner as the organizations they audit. An auditor can use benchmarking to shed much needed light on questionable performance and help the auditee find opportunities to improve performance. The audit report should focus on motivating effective performance rather than criticizing poor performance.

We end our book with Chapter Eleven, "Conclusion." Here, we challenge the practitioner and academic communities to research unexplored aspects of benchmarking. As yet, there is no taxonomy of benchmarking results or sufficient research to substantiate the degree of correlation between implementation of best practices and performance improvement. Chapter Eleven also reviews some of the basic benchmarking steps in order to assist the reader in getting started with a benchmarking project.

Benchmarking for Improving Accountability

The degree to which citizens trust the public and nonprofit sectors carries significant consequences. When citizens lose trust in government, elected officials are replaced, taxes are scrutinized more closely, and public support for government projects wanes. Likewise, when the general public lacks trust in the nonprofit sector, development projects are much more difficult to accomplish. Accountability and transparency are directly linked to perceptions of trust. The general public has proven repeatedly that they are willing to support the public and nonprofit sectors with their money—if they can count on those organizations to be accountable. Unfortunately, too often the public trust is damaged.

The lack of accountability and oversight at Enron and WorldCom led to the financial demise of hundreds if not thousands of hard-working, middle-class individuals and families in the United States. Halliburton executives' inability to answer questions about how billions of taxpayers' dollars were spent in Iraq is one of the reasons public support for the current federal administration is dropping. The FBI and the CIA have been criticized for not effectively communicating to each other and the public prior to the terrorist attacks of 9/11 (U.S. Department of Justice, Office of Inspector General, 2004). Even leaders and decision makers for the American Red Cross have been scrutinized for managing their resources poorly (Walden, 2005).

It is imperative that members of local, national, and global communities hold public and nonprofit executives accountable for their actions in managing their organizations. Why? Because everyone's personal and financial circumstances and physical security may be directly linked to the ability to hold officials accountable for their decisions. We believe that it is vital to benchmark for accountability and thereby avoid some of the disastrous consequences that people and organizations experience when decision makers do not assume responsibility.

WHAT IS ACCOUNTABILITY?

By *accountability* we mean the principle that individuals and organizations are responsible for their actions and decisions. The public expects those individuals and organizations to conform to rules, regulations, and in some instances, common sense. When leaders' or executives' actions or decisions deviate from the rules or appear questionable, people have a right to ask that those behaviors and decisions be explained. Explanations that fall short can result in unpleasant consequences for the irresponsible person or organization, such as termination of employment, withholding of funds, formal inquiries or legal action, unwanted media attention, turnover in elected officials, poor audit reports, or a variety of other actions.

> *Accountability is the principle that individuals and organizations are responsible for their actions and decisions. When actions and decisions appear questionable, the public has the right to ask that those behaviors be explained.*

Like it or not, accountability has become a normal part of life in a government or nonprofit organization. Accountability is at the heart of a democratic regime that responds to the priorities of the public. Officials and executives may view accountability as a threat—auditors investigate them, performance measures declare their inefficiencies, the press is always looking for a good investigative story; and jokes about their shortcomings are rampant on the Internet. But accountability is not all bad from the organizational viewpoint.

INCREASED ATTENTION TO ACCOUNTABILITY

Increased attention to accountability has manifested itself in several ways. First, the federal government watchdog known for eighty-three years as the U.S. General Accounting Office (GAO) changed its name in 2004 to the U.S. Government

Accountability Office. The name was changed to better reflect this office's role in ensuring the efficient and effective performance of government agencies and in preventing such failures in accountability as those found at Enron and World-Com. As a leader in program and performance evaluation, policy analysis, and auditing, the GAO has clearly communicated its strong interest in truth and transparency through such a significant change in its name.

Additionally, in 2002, the Sarbanes-Oxley Act was signed into federal law, largely in response to a number of corporate accounting scandals. The intent of this law is to reinstate some level of public confidence in the accounting processes of corporations. This Act, sponsored by Senator Paul Sarbanes (D-MD) and Representative Michael Oxley (R-OH), was passed with near unanimous support—423 to 3 in the House and 99 to 0 in the Senate. The provisions of this law are directed primarily toward publicly traded corporations; however, they are also serving as a warning to many nonprofit organizations' managers. Moreover, this federal legislation is not alone in serving as an accountability wake-up call; a number of states have passed similar pieces of legislation.

Nonprofit leaders should look carefully at the provisions of Sarbanes-Oxley, as well as their state laws, and determine whether their organizations ought to voluntarily adopt governance best practices, even if not mandated by law.

—Independent Sector (2006, p. 2)

In addition to the Sarbanes-Oxley Act, the U.S. Congress has directly addressed accountability in the nonprofit sector. In 2004, the chairman of the Senate Finance Committee, Senator Chuck Grassley (R-IA), and that committee's ranking member, Senator Max Baucus (D-MT), sent a letter to the Independent Sector, a coalition of over six hundred nonprofit organizations, requesting the creation of an independent group of leaders from the nonprofit sector to consider and recommend actions to strengthen governance, ethical conduct, and accountability in public charities and private foundations. The Independent Sector was founded in 1980 and "provides a leadership forum for charities, foundations, and corporate giving programs committed to advancing the common good in America and around the world" (Independent Sector, 2007).

Additionally, the media and the Internet quickly notify most Americans of any questionable performance of elected or career public officials or nonprofit leaders and managers. Cell phones and text messaging, e-mail, blogs, and twenty-four-hour news channels bring instant information to members of the public about even the smallest missteps of public officials. We began this book by suggesting that it was the impact of technology on people's lives that necessitated this second edition. This technology is perhaps most evident in the speed at which people now receive information about public and nonprofit sector performance. Rapid communication dramatically increases the public's attention to fraud or suspicious spending, program failures, and transgressions of public officials, and that is not likely to change in the future.

Similarly, diverse broadcast and cable networks bring dozens of political commentary programs to people's homes. One survey of college students found that students get more political news from comedian and political satirist Jon Stewart than they do elsewhere (Shister, 2007).

Does benchmarking have a role in helping the public hold organizations and elected and career officials accountable for their actions? The answer to that question is surely yes. We believe benchmarking should be used to improve performance, not simply identify low performance, even though the discovery of poor performance is a necessary consequence of benchmarking. When used in a positive manner, benchmarking can be a very effective way to hold public and nonprofit entities accountable for the services that they provide, the products that they create for the public, and the way that they spend money.

HOW BENCHMARKING CONTRIBUTES TO ACCOUNTABILITY

We suggest that benchmarking can give a new, more positive spin to accountability. Observing the last couple of decades of organizations' benchmarking experience, we have learned that the benchmarking process can lead to numerous accountability-related benefits. In this chapter we focus on six specific benefits:

- Fiscal transparency
- Increased internal accountability

- Improved public relations

- Better preparation for a crisis

- Enhanced decision making

- Creation of a learning organization

Fiscal Transparency

One of the most frequently discussed aspects of public and nonprofit accountability is fiscal transparency. For example, nonprofit organizations are required to file an annual information form (Form 990) with the Internal Revenue Service, detailing their financial activities and operations. The completed forms are available to the general public and are becoming more and more easily accessible. For example, GuideStar is an organization that provides an on-line database of financial information on nonprofit organizations, primarily using data from 990 forms. The mission of GuideStar is to "revolutionize philanthropy and nonprofit practice by providing information that advances transparency, enables users to make better decisions, and encourages charitable giving" (GuideStar, 2007). Individuals make over eight million visits to this GuideStar database each year. Such open and complete sharing of financial data also creates a forum in which organizations can discuss management practices in an effort to search for best practices. Fiscal transparency reduces some potential hurdles to collecting data to begin a benchmarking project. Much of the required research data can be easily accessed and shared.

Fiscal transparency is also an important issue for many government organizations. State and local governments in recent years have embraced the idea of not just opening their financial books but of making the information more understandable and user friendly for citizens. A great example of a user-friendly budget is the Citizen's Budget document provided by Park City Municipal Corporation (a city participating in the Resort Community Benchmarking Project, discussed in Chapter Six). This document is created by the city "to provide residents and other interested parties with a simple, concise, and understandable overview of Park City's budget" (Park City, 2007). A number of state and municipal government entities across the nation are taking the same approach. Additionally, many government entities recognize the need to improve accountability by comparing costs to other private and public entities. The 2001 budget document for the city of San Diego highlights the importance of fiscal transparency and the need for benchmarking performance (Segal & Summers, 2002).

An important pillar in becoming the "First Great City of the Twenty-First Century" is the commitment to implement a continuous, systematic process for evaluating the quality and cost of services and products delivered by the city and comparing them with private and public industry leaders.

—City of San Diego, *Final Fiscal Year 2001 Budget*
(quoted in Segal & Summers, 2002, p. 1)

As we discussed earlier, the mass interconnectivity of the Internet and Web 2.0 has created a number of forums in which organizations can share information and improve their transparency. In 2007 alone, state legislatures in Kansas, Hawaii, Oklahoma, Texas, and Minnesota passed legislation to improve state government fiscal transparency. These bills were primarily directed to the use of the Internet to share information. For example, Hawaii's legislature just passed a law (HB 122) that requires the state Department of Budget and Finance to create and maintain a free Web site that discloses information on all state grants and contracts. Also in 2007, Missouri governor Matt Blunt signed an executive order creating the Missouri Accountability Portal (MAP). This Web site allows taxpayers to review how their tax money is being spent, tracking expenditures by category, vendor, and contract. These are just two of the recent examples of governments that are attempting to enhance accountability through improved budget and fiscal transparency.

Increased Internal Accountability

Benchmarking can increase internal accountability. Benchmarking is all about making comparisons and holding oneself or one's organization accountable for improving performance. As an organization benchmarks and reports performance to oversight and stakeholder groups, it gains credibility and engenders confidence that management is open to questions about its operations and actions. The U.S. Postal Service regularly benchmarks its processes, costs, and prices with the private sector. The use of adhesive stamps is an interesting example. In 2000, President Bill Clinton issued Executive Order 13148, directed toward federal environmental leadership and calling for, among other things, the use of "environmentally benign pressure sensitive adhesive labels." In response to the popularity of no-lick postage and the incentive to recycle, the U.S. Postal Service "asked representatives of the paper and pulp, adhesive, and converting industries to work with the U.S. Department of Agriculture's Forest Products Laboratory to address the root cause of 'stickies' [problem-causing adhesives and glues] and develop a solution." A benchmarking partnership was created. "In 2001, this public-private partnership fulfilled its mandate with the release of USPS P1238-F, which details specifications for postage stamps with 'environmentally benign adhesives'" (Office of the Federal Environmental Executive, 2007).

Additionally, in 2006, the U.S. Congress passed the Postal Accountability and Enhancement Act (PAEA). In compliance with PAEA, the U.S. Postal Service Office of Inspector General is required to detail and assess postal service efforts to improve workplace safety, reduce workplace-related injuries, and identify opportunities for improvement. After establishing internal benchmarks the U.S. Postal Service has been able to reduce the rate of injuries by over 25 percent through the last five years (U.S. Postal Service Office of Inspector General, 2007). Benchmarking played a key role in improved internal accountability for the U.S. Postal Service.

Improved Public Relations

Benchmarking creates an opportunity to report favorable performance in context and improve public relations. Numerous benchmarking examples in the private sector have focused on improving public relations or customer satisfaction. One of the most remarkable public sector examples that we came across was an effort to improve public relations in Lake County, Indiana.

Lake County is the second most populous county in the state of Indiana. In 2004, elected officials in this area faced an extremely upset constituency due to an unprecedented increase in land values and, likewise, an unprecedented increase in property taxes. A complex scenario led to a 700 to 800 percent tax increase for some Lake County businesses and residents. Needless to say, the county had a very difficult public relations problem to solve.

Lake County residents asked hundreds of questions about who benefited and who suffered from reassessment and from changes in the property tax credits and deductions. This process led to additional questions about whether the cost of local government in Lake County was too high. In response a team was created to conduct the Lake County Government Finance Study. The purpose of this study was to carefully and accurately address the issues of local government finance and specifically the use of property tax revenues. The study team worked hard to ensure that all its findings were accessible to the public. In addition to the final 120-page study report, twenty articles discussing the finance issue were published in local papers. This significant effort helped to explain a technical and complex system of taxation to the general public and in the end improved public relations significantly.

For change to take place, citizens, government officials and business leaders of Lake County must first have meaningful data and analyses so that they can make sound, informed decisions about the future. We look forward to continuing the database of tax and financial data we have built and using it as a benchmarking and analysis tool for other counties as well.

—Jerry Conover, director of the Indiana Business Research Center, a partner in the Lake County Government Finance Study ("New Study Looks at Property Taxes," 2005)

Better Preparation for a Crisis

Benchmarking can help people and organizations be better prepared to meet crises. Crises can occur in the public and private sectors for a variety of reasons. The economy could swing into a downturn resulting in financial strain, or a natural disaster could cause significant unanticipated damages and costs. Regardless of the type of crisis, it usually leads to one problem, unintended costs (or unexpected revenue loss). The most important element in successfully addressing a crisis is being prepared, or at least feeling prepared. "Be Prepared" is as imperative for organizations as it is for Boy Scouts when it comes to dealing appropriately with a crisis. Unfortunately, being prepared is much easier said than done.

A key activity for entities striving to prepare is to find another entity that has already learned from a crisis situation. In addition, it is sometimes necessary for organizations to prepare for a number of potential crisis situations and to evaluate several what-if scenarios. Each potential crisis situation provides a learning opportunity. Security and event managers constantly train and compare best practices for crisis situations. The media often gravitate to instances of administrative failure, but there are many examples of positive management in the face of trying circumstances. Most managers and executives hope that they never have to apply the best practices they have found to solve a crisis. However, a crisis can often be turned into an opportunity. For one example of this situation, we turn to the current health and obesity crisis in America.

Many studies in the last decade have focused on the rising percentage of obese children in the United States. In 2003, then U.S. surgeon general Richard Carmona addressed this issue for the U.S. House of Representatives. In his testimony, he said: "As Surgeon General, I welcome this chance to talk with you about a health crisis affecting every state, every city, every community, and every school across our great nation. The crisis is obesity. It's the fastest-growing cause of disease and death in America. And it's completely preventable" (Carmona, 2003). Government entities and the nonprofit sector have sought potential solutions to this crisis. One organization, Shaping America's Youth (SAY), has sought to centralize information and create a national dialogue. In partnership with the surgeon general, national health organizations, and the private sector, SAY has created a forum for organizations (public, private, and nonprofit) to share ideas, data, and best practices. The executive director for SAY, David McCarron, recently described its benchmarking efforts: "The 2,500 programs registered with SAY's online database have not only made an invaluable impact on the nation's effort to combat childhood obesity at the community level, as recently noted by the Institute of Medicine, it has provided a critical benchmark of our nation's effectiveness at solving this crisis" (Shaping America's Youth, 2006). This is an excellent example of three things that we have emphasized earlier (and frequently): (a) the power of collaboration through benchmarking to solve problems, (b) the importance of networks to facilitate benchmarking, and (c) the value of the Internet as a resource for sharing information. These aspects of benchmarking illustrate how the public, private, and nonprofit sectors are working together to turn a crisis situation into a positive opportunity.

Enhanced Decision Making and the Creation of a Learning Organization

All the previous accountability-related benefits of benchmarking culminate in enhanced decision making and the creation of a learning organization. The decision-making process is enhanced through benchmarking—we are convinced of that. When decision makers have options in the form of best practices, the choices that they make are more likely to be successful. When decision makers can measure their performance through benchmarking, efficiency is achieved and overall performance improves internally, externally, and in the face of crisis situations.

Most important, benchmarking helps an organization become a learning organization. Organizations that use benchmarking methodologies regularly evaluate their processes and performance measures and incorporate best practices into their own systems. This activity helps employees to develop skills that allow them to adapt to a changing environment. When new laws are passed, programs begin or end, or new administrators are appointed, a learning organization is adept at adjusting and moving on. Learning organizations are also well equipped to anticipate future challenges and to learn from past experiences. Regardless of the sector, organizations that become stagnant can quickly become inefficient or produce a poor service for their patrons.

Indeed, accountability is a serious concern for public and nonprofit organizations. The pressure to satisfy citizens and to deliver quality services at a limited cost requires that organizations continually learn and adapt. Benchmarking therefore becomes an essential tool for learning and is vital to ensuring accountability and avoiding some of the disastrous consequences that people and organizations experience when decision makers do not conform to expected rules or behaviors.

SUMMARY

- Accountability has taken center stage in the past ten years because of circumstances resulting from lack of accountability.

- Accountability asks individuals and organizations to explain activities and decisions that do not conform to expected rules or behaviors.

- Benchmarking improves accountability through fiscal transparency and increased internal accountability.

- Benchmarking improves public relations and helps an organization prepare for crises.

- Decision makers have more and better options when best practices are discovered through benchmarking.

- Organizations learn to research and to adapt to changing environments by benchmarking for best practices.

Use Worksheet 9.1, in the Resources, to evaluate your own organization's accountability.

Benchmarking and Performing an Audit

From engineers to accountants, from city managers to federal executives, and from government to nonprofit employees, all professions seem to come into contact with benchmarking concepts, tools, and techniques. Why then carve out a chapter especially for auditors? Two reasons—auditors are in a unique position to recommend benchmarking projects when organizations are performing poorly. Also, auditors are skilled at many tasks required for benchmarking projects.

Managers and staff of government and nonprofit organizations typically have an area of expertise—whether it is financial management, transportation, health or human services, safety, utilities, or one of the numerous other areas—with the result that each individual often has a *stovepipe,* or somewhat narrow, view of the organization. This limited perspective is especially common in larger organizations, where managers and staff tend to focus, and rightly so, on their immediate department's performance and may have an opportunity to serve on benchmarking teams only within their scope of responsibility or their area's boundaries.

Conversely, the auditor frequently works across internal boundaries as he or she completes various audits. Working across boundaries gives the auditor a different perspective of an organization's performance. In the course of one program audit, the auditor often has a chance to see different performance levels in different geographical or departmental locations. Seeing these various performance levels, the auditor may be prompted to recommend that the agency conduct a benchmarking study or may be able to report some promising practices. In some instances, auditors can play a unique role by conducting or recommending benchmarking projects, even though they are not responsible for the process or problem to be addressed. Organizations are obligated to consider any auditor recommendations closely. It is this uniqueness that warrants special attention.

Many auditors also possess some of the important skills necessary for a successful benchmarking project. Most public or nonprofit professionals have probably come in contact with an auditor. Auditors are often nice people, but they are not always enthusiastically welcomed in many public or nonprofit organizations. The auditor's job is to identify problems and failures and to recommend ways to correct these situations. It sounds easy to criticize a program or agency—after all, most people have clear opinions and wonderful ideas about how government and nonprofit agencies should be run—but in fact auditors follow systematic and reliable methods to ensure that the problems they find are well documented. Auditors also must clearly demonstrate the extent to which those problems are impeding an organization's performance. The auditing profession has established guidelines that ensure that auditors are well trained in some fundamental skills and that audit findings are consistently developed in terms of the five elements of a finding. An auditor's training and skill and the defined structure of findings ensure that any recommendation that an auditor makes to benchmark is well grounded in evidence and analysis.

WHY USE BENCHMARKING IN AUDITS?

Like many professionals in public and nonprofit organizations, many auditors have sought and received training in how to conduct benchmarking projects. The Graduate School, USDA, Government Audit Training Institute (GATI) offered a course titled "Performance Auditing: A Benchmarking Approach," as early as 1996. Delivered to hundreds of auditors since, it was updated in 2006 at the request of the Office of Inspector General (OIG) of the U.S. Department of the Interior (DOI). The course materials offered four reasons that the training was desired.

1. The DOI's OIG and the Government Performance and Results Act of 1993 had established a performance goal of including best practices in an increasing number of products.

2. Benchmarking is viewed as a reliable method for seeking and identifying promising practices.

3. Benchmarking can assist agency officials with finding solutions to persistent problems.

4. The use of reliable and widely accepted methods such as benchmarking can add credibility to an audit report.

These are also the reasons why so many other audit offices are increasing their use of benchmarking tools and techniques. Fortunately, many auditors bring excellent skills to any benchmarking project.

BASIC BENCHMARKING SKILLS FOR AUDITORS

A good auditor must possess some fundamental skills in at least three key areas: research, data collection and analysis, and development of audit findings. When executing the audit program, auditors are frequently called on to read, comprehend, and summarize dozens of reports, memos, and other documents and to analyze data sets ranging from purchase orders to student test scores to health care costs. Anyone who enjoys snooping around asking questions such as, "Why did they do that?" or, "How did that happen?" or, "How can the program be improved?" should consider joining the audit profession. This natural or trained curiosity combined with an ability to research is exactly the skill that is important to benchmarking. Research means following a trail of information until questions are answered and curiosity is satisfied. Similarly, anyone using the benchmarking methodologies must research and understand (a) the practice, policy, process, or activity to be benchmarked; (b) the best practice or solution under consideration; and (c) the potential impact of implementing the best practice or solution. Auditors can apply their excellent research skills to benchmarking.

Auditors regularly collect and analyze many types of data. They receive extensive training in organizing and displaying data to ensure that both the data and its implications are easy to understand, regardless of the true complexity of the audit findings. Audit reports are read by many uninformed readers who may not have the time or inclination to delve into the complicated details. Auditors are well positioned to use benchmarking methodologies because they often have a strong ability to analyze and display data in a simple yet meaningful way.

Auditors are trained to develop five elements of a finding:

- Criteria
- Condition
- Effect
- Cause
- Recommendations

The *criteria* establish the standards, goals, or expectations for organizational or program performance. The *condition* is simply the current performance level or practice(s). Auditors often develop evidence that demonstrates the difference between the criteria and the condition. This evidence is called an *effect*. In benchmarking the effect is the gap in performance between the benchmarking organization and the partner organization. The *cause* of the performance gap is also developed during the program audit, and in the case of benchmarking, the cause of the performance difference is presumably the failure to use the best practice used by the partner organization. *Recommendations* in audit reports are actions that should be taken by the organization to (a) improve performance or (b) eliminate the cause of the effect.

These elements of a finding provide the auditor with a framework for organizing the audit activities, analyzing results, and producing the audit report. The elements of a finding can be applied to both the traditional and solution-driven benchmarking methods, albeit in different ways, to ensure that the auditor gets the most from each method.

USING TRADITIONAL BENCHMARKING IN AUDITS

It is precisely their role as independent evaluators of an organization or program that prevents auditors from conducting a traditional benchmarking study during an audit. The auditing agency is, by definition, independent and separate from the auditee, the organization being audited. Therefore, auditors do not have the authority or responsibility to charter a benchmarking team within the auditee. Neither do auditors have the day-to-day interaction with auditee staff to collect data or to fully understand the process under scrutiny. Moreover, auditors are separate from the auditee and therefore cannot oversee the day-to-day implementation of best practices. Hence, an auditor cannot incorporate the traditional benchmarking method into an audit program.

Auditors can, however, use the traditional benchmarking method in three ways. First, auditors can apply the traditional method to their own audit process. For example, most audit offices track the length of time that they take to complete various portions of the audit program and the overall time that they take to produce a report. Benchmarking the process and cycle times can reveal opportunities to streamline the audit process. Using the traditional method to do this benchmarking would be appropriate.

Consider the example of the Association of Local Government Auditors (ALGA), formerly known as the National Association of Local Government Auditors (NALGA). NALGA conducted benchmarking and best practices surveys from 1996 to 2000. It compiled comparative data such as staff size, budget, and cost per audit hour for participating audit offices. It also surveyed audit offices to determine which offices were implementing the best practices through the years of the study. Offices reported an increase in some best practices, such as conducting external peer reviews (from 30 percent in 1996 to 52 percent in 2002) and using customer surveys (from 32 percent in 1996 to 42 percent in 2002). The implementation of other promising practices declined: for example, use of a formal risk assessment document went from 72 percent in 1996 to 62 percent in 2002 (ALGA, 2002).

A second way that auditors can use traditional benchmarking is to develop findings. If the auditee has completed a benchmarking study, the auditor can evaluate how the auditee applied the benchmarking process and the results of the study. Here's how it would be done. First auditors must ask about the process completed by the benchmarking team. Did the team comply with established benchmarking methods while completing the study? Use this book or other reliable sources of benchmarking methodologies as criteria for the auditee's benchmarking process. Check to see whether the agency's benchmarking team followed the methodology or deviated significantly. Significant variations from a proven method could lead to other problems.

Additionally, auditors must develop three *conditions*: the condition prior to the agency's benchmarking study, the condition immediately after the benchmarking, and the condition at least six months after full implementation of the best practice, or the most current performance. The difference among these conditions will clearly demonstrate the *effect*. Hopefully the trend will show improved performance, thus demonstrating the *cause* is likely to have been the best or promising practice.

The traditional benchmarking method requires that the benchmarking team clearly defines the process or function selected for improvement. Frequently the team creates flowcharts and collects data to establish baseline performance. It accumulates numerous notes, spreadsheets, compilations of data, and minutes from team meetings for later use in the study. The agency will also have performance information after implementation. Hence the auditor can obtain these team documents or refer to the final report to develop the elements of a finding.

An example is found in the May 2007 U.S. Government Accountability Office (GAO) report on the Federal Retirement Thrift Investment Board (FRTIB). GAO reviewed several administrative functions, including a benchmarking study of the costs of administrative expenses (U.S. Government Accountability Office, 2007). The GAO report criticized the benchmarking methods followed by FRTIB because it resulted in incomplete information. Further, GAO suggested that FRTIB overlooked some important potential partners in other federal agencies. An auditor must be familiar with benchmarking methodologies in order to evaluate agencies that use them.

A third way to use the traditional benchmarking method is to recommend that the organization or program undertake such a study. If it appears that the organization's performance is consistently problematic, the auditor should consider whether a traditional benchmarking study would help management identify ways to improve (see the chapters in Part Two that discuss preparing for benchmarking and selecting an appropriate method). If it seems desirable and if evidence substantiates it, auditors can recommend a process that the organization should benchmark. In July 2005, for example, the GAO chastised the Internal Revenue Service for failing to benchmark, to find best practices, and to improve the accuracy of information provided to taxpayers. One final recommendation was that the IRS benchmark training and development programs against high-performing organizations (U.S. Government Accountability Office, 2005).

A side benefit of the traditional benchmarking method is that the auditee's staff must define and analyze the current process. It is common for a benchmarking team to streamline and improve the process before the study is completed. So the benchmarking method may provide some interim relief and improvements prior to the team's final report.

In summary, auditors follow their customary audit procedures when it comes to the traditional benchmarking methodology. Audit findings can be developed from agency benchmarking reports, and auditors can recommend that agencies complete traditional benchmarking projects. The only time an auditor completes a traditional benchmarking study is when that study is applied to processes within the audit agency.

USING SOLUTION-DRIVEN BENCHMARKING IN AUDITS

In stark contrast to being able only to employ or to recommend traditional benchmarking, the auditor can play an active role when using the solution-driven method (see Table 10.1). With the exception of implementing the promising practice (step 4: Import Solutions), auditors can complete an entire solution-driven study as part of the audit program. How does this work? First, let's assume that the auditor is going to complete a solution-driven benchmarking study and link the results to the elements of a finding.

Table 10.1
Auditors' Roles in Traditional and Solution-Driven Benchmarking

TRADITIONAL	SOLUTION-DRIVEN
Participate in benchmarking of the audit process within the agency being audited.	Prompt discovery by clearly demonstrating the condition.
Evaluate benchmarking studies completed by the agency to determine compliance with the methodology, effective use of agency resources, and results.	Establish or promote criteria through background research. Search for promising practices and demonstrate a performance gap (cause and effect).
Recommend that the agency complete a traditional study.	Recommend promising practices for implementation by the agency being audited.

The first step in the solution-driven method is the discovery of the problem that prompts the search for a promising practice (see Table 10.2). The problem, once documented, is the *condition*. The auditor could complete this step as part of the planning or scoping phase of an audit (these phases are discussed later in this chapter). By reviewing prior reports or other existing documents, the auditor can give the problem a framework or substance. The auditor can use this step to prompt discovery in the organization. If the problem is serious enough, and the auditor meets with organization officials, the problem may gain significant

Table 10.2
Elements of a Finding in Relation to Benchmarking Steps in Each Method

TRADITIONAL BENCHMARKING STEPS	ELEMENT OF A FINDING
1. Charter a team.	
2. Determine the purpose and scope of the benchmarking initiative.	
3. Clearly define the process or function you intend to benchmark.	Condition
4. Research potential benchmarking partners.	
5. Choose performance measures.	
6. Collect internal data to establish baseline performance.	Condition
7. Collect data from the partner organization.	Criteria
8. Analyze the performance gap between processes.	Cause and effect
9. Import practices in order to close the performance gap.	Recommendation
10. Regularly monitor results after implementing changes.	
11. Reevaluate changes and start anew.	

SOLUTION-DRIVEN BENCHMARKING STEPS	ELEMENT OF A FINDING
1. Discover the problem.	Condition
2. Establish criteria for solutions.	Criteria
3. Search for promising practices.	
4. Implement promising practices.	Cause and effect; recommendation
5. Monitor progress.	

attention before the full audit is underway. This can be a good thing, although it may steal some thunder from the audit report.

The second step is to establish *criteria* for solutions. Measures or other criteria lay out and define success and what is expected to result from the promising practice. By completing step 2, the auditor develops the criteria that must be established for an audit finding. If desired, the auditor can offer the criteria to the organization's officials who are responsible for the problem or process and ask, "Is it unreasonable to expect your organization to resolve the problem or improve performance in this manner?"

The third step in the solution-driven method is to search for promising practices. The auditor's research skills are put to the test during this step. As discussed in Chapter Five, this is when the benchmarking individual, or in this case the auditor, scours the Internet and other sources for information on best practices related to the process or the problem. The auditor may also be a member of a professional association or have a personal contact that could yield ideas for promising practices. The auditor should be prepared to meet with some resistance during this step. Organizations are not always motivated to help an auditor. The idea of disclosing information to an auditor can be somewhat threatening even though the discussion may be about best practices located in the organization. In some cases the audit supervisor may need to use personal contacts or the power of position and authority to help connect audit staff with other federal staff who have information about promising practices.

The fourth step, implementing promising practices, cannot be completed by the auditor for the same reasons that the auditor cannot complete a traditional benchmarking study. The auditor does not have the authority or the responsibility necessary to adapt and install a new practice. Auditors can, however, complete the fifth step of monitoring progress. They can periodically review organizations to determine whether previous recommendations (of best or promising practices) from the solution-driven benchmarking study have been implemented.

AN EXAMPLE FROM THE DOI

In one of its early uses of solution-driven benchmarking, the U.S. Department of the Interior Office of Inspector General (2004) reviewed the fleet management operations throughout the department. Embedded in the OIG's audit report are the components of the solution-driven method and elements of a finding. In the background section of the report, the problem is discovered and brought to light. In 2002, over $200 million was spent on 36,000 vehicles, yet many of those vehicles were underused, costing the department an estimated $34 million each year. The report establishes criteria for success (and for the finding) by citing the Bureau of Land Management's utilization rate of about 90 percent, whereas other rates were as low as 39 percent.

The search for promising practices included comparisons to two non-DOI federal agencies, two state agencies, two universities, and the U.S. General Services Administration. The DOI's Office of Inspector General auditors contacted other federal agencies recognized for their high performance in fleet management to identify best practices. In some cases the agency officials were reluctant to take the time or to share information. However, ultimately, the search yielded five best practices, which were incorporated into the recommendations. The solution-driven benchmarking methodology was well integrated into the audit steps and the final audit report.

WARNINGS ABOUT THE SOLUTION-DRIVEN METHOD

Auditors should use a bit of caution when recommending that organizations adopt best or promising practices discovered through solution-driven benchmarking. In the traditional benchmarking method the best practices are closely scrutinized before being adapted to the benchmarking organization. This does not happen in the solution-driven method. The auditor does not closely examine a best practice prior to implementation because that would require a completely new audit of the promising practice within the partner organization. The auditor can, however, help the organization to identify questions that it should consider before implementing the practice:

- Does this best practice require unique hardware or software to implement?

- Are staff appropriately trained to incorporate this new practice into day-to-day work processes?

- If implemented, will this best practice violate any existing policies or laws?

- Have we attempted to implement this practice in the past? If so, what is different that will ensure success this time?

Auditors can undoubtedly play a significant role in improving an organization's performance through the solution-driven benchmarking method.

SOLUTION-DRIVEN BENCHMARKING AND THE AUDIT PLAN

Another advantage of the solution-driven method is that the auditor can apply the method at various points throughout the audit. If the audit is likely to include solution-driven benchmarking, the benchmarking steps must be integrated into the normal audit plan. The Government Auditing Standards (U.S. Government Accountability Office, 2003) establish standards and guidelines for various audit steps. The following is the standard for audit steps and a few questions that an auditor manager should answer when developing an audit plan that involves benchmarking.

Plan

Work should be "adequately planned." The audit plan should include audit objectives, scope, and methods. Planning is a continuous process. Therefore auditors should consider whether they need to adjust the objectives, scope, and methods as the audit progresses.

- Do I want to include solution-driven benchmarking in this audit?

- If so, at what point in the audit should I develop promising practices? Scope? Data collection?

- Has the agency completed a traditional benchmarking study? If so, what were the results? Do I want to evaluate the traditional benchmarking study as part of my data collection and analysis?

The audit plan should explain why the audit will address best practices; one reason might be an agency's consistently poor performance. The plan should also include a brief description of how solution-driven benchmarking is expected to help the agency with best practices. If a traditional benchmarking study conducted by the agency is to be reviewed, the audit plan should explain why it is important to review the study.

Objectives

The objectives describe what the audit is intended to accomplish. These objectives include the audit subject and the performance aspects to be included. Audit objectives may be seen as questions that the audit is intended to answer.

- What performance measure(s) indicate that the organization or program has performed poorly?
- Would solution-driven benchmarking contribute to the audit's objectives? If so, how?
- What problem or process do I hope will be improved by my identification of best or promising practices?

Scope

The scope defines the parameters of the audit, such as the period of time reviewed and the documents, records, locations, or other limits directly linked to the audit objectives.

- If I am to include best or promising practices in the audit, how many organizations do I want to include in the comparison?
- What time period will I consider? One year? Two years?
- If the organization has numerous geographical locations, which ones should be included in the audit?

Staff

Audits should be adequately staffed by individuals who possess the appropriate knowledge and experience to meet the objectives.

- Have my staff been trained on benchmarking methods? If so, are they available to work on my audit? For what period of time?

- Have any of my staff participated in traditional or solution-driven benchmarking? If so, are they available to work on my audit? If not, when can I interview them to identify lessons learned from their experience?

- Do I have enough staff during the scoping activities to determine whether the solution-driven methodology will be useful in the full audit?

Data Collection and Analysis

Data must be collected from reliable and valid sources of information.

- Does the organization currently collect the data that could be used in a solution-driven benchmarking study? Are these data readily available?

- What are the top seven or eight sources of potential best or promising practices, such as other agencies, the Internet, or professional associations?

- Do the data clearly indicate poor performance that could be improved by implementing best or promising practices?

- Will the organization be able to demonstrate improved performance if it adopts best or promising practices?

- Will I need any special analytical tools for the solution-driven benchmarking methodology?

Recommendations

Use the elements of a finding (criteria, condition, cause, and effect) to help develop the recommendations.

- Will I need to develop evidence related to criteria?

- Do criteria already exist for expected or desired performance?

- Do I need to caution the organization to consider the best or promising practice carefully before implementing it?

- Does the organization need additional resources before it can implement the best or promising practice?

These questions are only a sample of the questions that must be asked to meet auditing standards when benchmarking is included in the audit process. An experienced auditor will note that most of these questions are fundamental to virtually all audits. The solution-driven benchmarking method does not require a significant adjustment of an audit plan or of work steps.

SUMMARY

- Auditors should be familiar with both benchmarking methodologies as tools for finding promising practices.
- Auditors are not likely to conduct a traditional benchmarking study, but they can recommend it to their auditees.
- Reports from benchmarking teams within organizations can provide auditors with several elements of a finding and opportunities to reinforce or dispute recommendations.
- Auditors can complete all the steps in a solution-driven benchmarking study except for implementing the promising practices.
- Auditors must be cautious when recommending solutions and promising practices because they are not responsible for implementing or monitoring them.

Use Worksheets 10.1, 10.2, and 10.3, in the Resources, for assistance in working with solution-driven benchmarking in performing an audit.

Conclusion

This book does not offer the final word on benchmarking. Benchmarking is evolving—so, too, are the ideas in this book. Yet the research and cases presented here clearly demonstrate the widespread use of benchmarking in the public and nonprofit sectors. Benchmarking for best practices essentially is sharing ideas. Never before have organizations of all kinds collaborated and shared ideas to the extent that they have in the early twenty-first century. The rise of the knowledge and information age coupled with the proven successes of benchmarking make the search for best practices a common pursuit for many nonprofit and public organizations. Technology gives managers and staff immediate and easy access to other people, places, organizations, and experiences throughout the world, providing them with a vast amount of information and resources.

However, benchmarking is *not* a panacea, the solution to all problems that public and nonprofit sectors face. It is a powerful tool to improve performance, but the process needs to be carried beyond the steps of implementation. Before success can be claimed, best practices need to be monitored and measured. Realtors' mantra is said to be "location, location, location"—and we contend that anyone interested in benchmarking should take up the mantra "measure, measure, measure." Keep asking yourself, "Where is the proof that this works?" Monitoring sometimes evokes negative connotations, but monitoring is intended to be a positive learning experience. Creating and fostering an organizational culture of learning is a significant key to shifting monitoring from a negative to a positive experience.

SUSTAINING THE MOMENTUM FOR BENCHMARKING: CREATING A LEARNING ORGANIZATION

The success of a benchmarking process is often only as strong as the momentum that sustains the process. As we discussed in earlier chapters, many stakeholders must be invested in and must maintain commitment to the project for the momentum to carry through to the monitoring stage. In our experience, it is clear that this momentum is often directly linked to the degree to which an organization is a learning organization. In the previous edition of this book, we discussed a simple model for organizational learning—that model still rings true.

There are four stages in the learning process. In the first stage—the initial experience—the benchmarking participants undoubtedly make some mistakes, have some unexpected successes, and encounter new challenges and surprises. These experiences should not be taken lightly; they are the basis for organizational learning.

During the second stage of the learning process, the benchmarking participants individually and collectively reflect on what these experiences, trials, and accomplishments mean to them, the organization, the clients, and the constituents. The culture of the organization is now one marked by a continual search for improvement and an eager willingness to share best practices with partner organizations. The drive for excellence in one organization feeds a similar drive in the other organizations.

When participants can reflect on and understand a benchmarking experience, the organization is ready to make decisions about how to improve the process. This third stage of learning requires that participants carefully evaluate the process. As we have indicated throughout this book, there is no single, perfect process for benchmarking. To determine for themselves what process works best, benchmarking participants will need to determine the time and resources that they have available to invest in the project. Again, we emphasize that either a formal (step-by-step) process or a less traditional solution-driven approach can unveil best practices, enabling improved performance.

New processes in an organization, just like new skills that an individual tries to master, require constant attention and continual practice. Sometimes an old practice must be unlearned (old habits must be broken), and the new process must be exercised until it becomes standard operating procedure. Too often benchmarking teams identify a best practice, but then, during the early implementation stage, team members fade back into their normal jobs and abandon the new practice. An organization misses a terrific opportunity to improve itself when it does not follow through with ongoing benchmarking activities for the new process. This is the final step in the learning process—a commitment to continue benchmarking and a willingness to be flexible and to adapt the process as needed.

CONDUCTING NEEDED RESEARCH

Despite the current affinity for benchmarking in the public and nonprofit sectors, our research for this book revealed several weaknesses in the literature, such as the lack of a benchmarking taxonomy and the lack of documented proven successes, which should be addressed in future research.

Develop a Benchmarking Taxonomy

We could not locate any publications that attempted to organize or categorize benchmarking studies. This gap may be due partially to benchmarking's relatively recent popularity. It is only in the past two decades that the number of organizations that are benchmarking has markedly increased. Now that many organizations have tried benchmarking and appear comfortable with the results, it is time to more closely examine these results.

It is possible that certain types of organizations within the government and nonprofit sectors tend to apply benchmarking in different ways or under different circumstances. For example, local governments may find it more useful to benchmark public works or financial management, and federal agencies may tend to benchmark customer service. Nonprofits may use the solution-driven method more than the traditional approach. All of this is somewhat unexplored. We suggest that research could effectively focus on the following questions:

- Do sectors or portions of sectors vary in their selection of benchmarking subjects?

- Can best practices be categorized or analyzed according to unique characteristics involving complexity, implementation, or the number of organizations involved in implementation?

- What evidence demonstrates a cause-and-effect relationship between benchmarking and improved performance?

- What is the true cost of benchmarking, especially when compared to the tangible benefits?

Public administrators and academicians in partnership need to address these questions as part of the continuous improvement of the benchmarking methodologies.

Seek Proven Successes

The causal links between benchmarking studies and improved performance are somewhat speculative. Despite award programs and dozens of Web sites that promote best practices, research on the link between benchmarking projects and improved performance is not particularly well developed. Most of the benchmarking literature is oriented toward assisting practitioners rather than reporting academic research, probably because of benchmarking's immediate application to the practitioner environment.

Many variables that could contribute to successful benchmarking studies remain unexplored. It is possible that the Hawthorne effect (that is, simply giving attention to a problem) results in success. To date, we have not found a meta-analysis that looks across benchmarking studies to determine the degree of successful results.

Explore the Solution-Driven Method Further

The solution-driven method needs to be further developed. We are excited to offer this methodology to you, but it is not as proven as the traditional method. The solution-driven method itself may or may not have matured, but the recognition and acknowledgment of this method is still in its infancy. Solution-driven benchmarking is a process that requires greater research and attention. We are not naïve about the potential dangers of this approach compared to the traditional approach. It is more risky for an organization to implement a promising practice without completely identifying potential challenges to success. And individuals and organizations may begin the implementation stage without winning the necessary buy-in from various stakeholders—without buy-in, implementation is at risk.

NEXT STEPS

The forces driving the public sector to find best practices have intensified in the last decade, and now those forces are affecting the nonprofit sector as well. We echo the same observation that we made ten years ago—the members of the American public demand excellence from their public and nonprofit organizations. In addition to meeting this demand for excellence, organization managers and executives must balance the responsibilities of accountability and efficiency with restricted or even shrinking budgets. The American public have a right to demand excellence and accountability for the taxes that they pay and the money that they charitably contribute. The pressure for managers and executives to perform is real and should be responded to with energy and focus.

Over the years we have worked with many organizations and watched many others as they tried to manage this pressure to perform. Some organizations withdraw into themselves. A bunker mentality sets in, and the world comes to be seen as divided between us and them. Other organizations turn outward, looking for help, ideas, and new perspectives from outside their own boundaries. Benchmarking encourages organizations to look outward. It provides the reasons and methods that organizations need to seek out best practices and solve their performance problems.

If you are ready to begin a benchmarking project, we suggest that you prepare yourself in the following ways: capitalize on the worksheets provided at the end of this book. They offer step-by-step guides that will help you ask the right questions, choose appropriate actions, and organize your project. And don't overlook the possibility of seeking formal training in how to benchmark. Numerous professional organizations offer such training at annual conferences for a reasonable price.

Expect to apply your organization's unique characteristics to the benchmarking process. Assume that benchmarking is iterative and that you will refer back to this book—network with others, move ahead, and bounce around a bit. Capitalize on the energy that comes with a bounce and with new insight. Most of all, *carefully* apply the benchmarking method to your project. Use common sense and professional judgment as you move through your project to adapt the methodology, no matter which one you chose, to your unique circumstances. We believe that both methods are sufficiently robust to accommodate virtually any topic or circumstance.

Do not hesitate to fail. We did not find any benchmarking studies that reported failure even though we are certain failures have occurred. Failure is acceptable only if the lessons learned are applied to future success.

Take the time to report your success. Magazines, newsletters, and Web pages that feature public and nonprofit organizations frequently encourage practitioners to publish their success stories. Professional organizations such as the Chamber of Commerce or Rotary Club often give governments or nonprofits the opportunity to tout their successes in chapter meetings. Benchmarking is about learning from others, so be sure to give another person or organization the opportunity to learn from you. Finally, be sure to relish your contribution to a learning organization.

RESOURCES

The worksheets in this resource will assist you in carrying out many benchmarking tasks. Note that the worksheet numbering corresponds to the chapter numbers. Also, the worksheets can be used in a two-day benchmarking workshop that is described in the Instructor's Guide at www.wiley.com/college/keehley.

Individuals and teams that are new to benchmarking should take the time to complete the worksheets in the sequence shown here. More experienced individuals and teams may wish to test their knowledge first by completing Worksheets 1.1 and 2.1, then proceed to Worksheet 3.2 to select the correct benchmarking method.

Auditors may wish to complete Worksheets 10.1 and 10.2 before including a benchmarking study in the audit process.

Worksheet I.1
Starting My Research

Instructions: Use this worksheet to determine where additional research will benefit your benchmarking project. Review each issue and write out the questions that you want to answer. Then review the information in the recommended chapter to find your answer.

If You're Looking For . . .	**Try Looking Here . . .**
1. Context and history	Chapter 1
My question:	Answer/Page #:
_____	_____
_____	_____
_____	_____
2. Relationship between training and benchmarking	Chapter 1
My question:	Answer/Page #:
_____	_____
_____	_____
_____	_____
3. Concepts and uses of performance measures	Chapter 2
My question:	Answer/Page #:
_____	_____
_____	_____
_____	_____
4. Relationship between performance measures and benchmarking	Chapter 2
My question:	Answer/Page #:
_____	_____
_____	_____
_____	_____

Worksheet I.1 (Continued)

5. Comparisons and conceptual differ-   Chapter 3
    ences between the methods

    My question: Answer/Page #:

    _____   _____

    _____   _____

    _____   _____

6. How to select a method   Chapter 3

    My question: Answer/Page #:

    _____   _____

    _____   _____

    _____   _____

7. Examples and instructions for using   Chapter 4
    the traditional benchmarking method

    My question: Answer/Page #:

    _____   _____

    _____   _____

    _____   _____

8. Examples and instructions for using   Chapter 5
    the solution-driven benchmarking
    method

    My question: Answer/Page #:

    _____   _____

    _____   _____

    _____   _____

9. Cases of benchmarking at the state   Chapter 6
    and local government levels

    My question: Answer/Page #:

    _____   _____

    _____   _____

    _____   _____

Worksheet I.1 (Continued)

10. Cases of benchmarking by nonprofits   Chapter 7

    My question: Answer/Page #:

    _____   _____

    _____   _____

    _____   _____

11. Cases of benchmarking throughout the world   Chapter 8

    My question: Answer/Page #:

    _____   _____

    _____   _____

    _____   _____

12. How benchmarking can improve accountability   Chapter 9

    My question: Answer/Page #:

    _____   _____

    _____   _____

    _____   _____

13. How auditors can use benchmarking   Chapter 10

    My question: Answer/Page #:

    _____   _____

    _____   _____

    _____   _____

14. How elements of a finding link to the benchmarking steps   Chapter 10

    My question: Answer/Page #:

    _____   _____

    _____   _____

    _____   _____

Worksheet I.1 (Continued)

15. Areas that need additional research   Chapter 11

    My question: Answer/Page #:

    _____   _____

    _____   _____

    _____   _____

16. Quick and easy steps to launch your   Chapter 11
    benchmarking project

    My question: Answer/Page #:

    _____   _____

    _____   _____

    _____   _____

17. Definitions of terms   Glossary

    My question: Answer/Page #:

    _____   _____

    _____   _____

    _____   _____

18. Worksheets to get you started and   Resources
    help you complete the benchmarking
    process

    My question: Answer/Page #:

    _____   _____

    _____   _____

    _____   _____

19. More information   Index

    My question: Answer/Page #:

    _____   _____

    _____   _____

    _____   _____

    Other notes:

Worksheet 1.1
Definitions and Basic Concepts

Instructions: Use this worksheet to review definitions and basic concepts.

1. A benchmark is _____

2. Benchmarking is _____

3. Name three performance improvement trends through which benchmarking remained intact.

   a. _____

   b. _____

   c. _____

4. Will benchmarking likely continue into this century? Why?

   _____

   _____

   _____

5. Name the two benchmarking methodologies and identify some of the major differences between them.

   a. _____

   b. _____

   Differences _____

   _____

   _____

   _____

   _____

Worksheet 1.1 (Continued)

6. Describe the relationship between training and benchmarking.

_____

_____

_____

7. What is a best practice? A promising practice?

_____

_____

_____

8. What concerns should I have when I read about a best practice?

_____

_____

_____

Worksheet 2.1
Learning Performance Measurement Language

Instructions: Define the following terms.

1. Measure _____

_____

2. Input _____

_____

3. Output _____

_____

4. Process _____

_____

5. Outcome _____

_____

6. Quality _____

_____

7. Efficiency _____

_____

8. Effectiveness _____

_____

9. Cycle time _____

_____

10. Customer satisfaction _____

_____

11. Error rate _____

_____

12. Timeliness _____

_____

Worksheet 2.1 (Continued)

13. Productivity _____

_____

14. Unit cost _____

_____

15. Customer _____

_____

16. Strategic goal _____

_____

Worksheet 2.2
Develop Measures for Your Organization's Process

Instructions: Work individually or in small groups as you develop performance measures for the process you are going to benchmark.

1. Identify the process that will be benchmarked. Give it a name:

   _____

2. Identify the beginning and end points that are under your control.

   a. Beginning point: _____

   b. End point: _____

3. Use Post-it notes to flow chart the process. Brainstorm a list of major process steps. Write one step on each Post-it. Organize the steps in a way that depicts the process flow.

4. Identify the points in the process where major performance measures are needed to monitor or manage performance. Determine whether measures currently exist for these areas.

5. Describe the primary customer of the process and the performance level expected by that customer.

   _____

   _____

   _____

6. Describe the current problems with the process. Use measures to clearly state deficits in performance.

   _____

   _____

   _____

Worksheet 2.2 (Continued)

7. Using the following diagram, categorize the performance measures and write each one in the appropriate box.

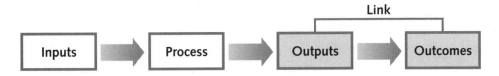

8. Determine whether these measures are good measures (see the following list of criteria). Are they valid, reliable, and useful indicators of the process performance? Can they be collected?

Criteria for Good Measures

- Valid: measures what it is supposed to measure (for example, a thermometer measures temperature not inches).

- Reliable: gives consistent measure over time (for example, a yardstick always measures distance in the same way regardless of the item—floor, wall, countertop—being measured).

- Useful: provides information that can be used by individuals, management, customers, auditors, or others.

- Collectable: the measures can be collected on a regular basis without an undue burden on individuals or the organization.

9. Identify the desired outcome or long-term goal to which this process contributes.

_____

_____

_____

Worksheet 2.3
Selecting Measures for the Benchmarking Study

Instructions: Use the following list of questions to evaluate whether the measures chosen for your benchmarking study are appropriate and available.

1.	The measures illustrate the current process performance or the magnitude of the problem.	Yes	No	Explain
2.	The measures accurately and appropriately illustrate the process or problem.	Yes	No	Explain
3.	The measures are readily available.	Yes	No	Explain
4.	Additional measures will be needed to conduct a benchmarking study.	Yes	No	Explain
5.	The data collection systems for the measures are reliable.	Yes	No	Explain
6.	The measures are used by potential partners.	Yes	No	Explain
7.	The date that each measure was collected and reported corresponds with the dates desired to benchmark the process or problem.	Yes	No	Explain
8.	The process or problem is represented by more than a single measure.	Yes	No	Explain
9.	The benchmarking team will have easy access to the measures.	Yes	No	Explain
10.	Reports on the measures will be readily available.	Yes	No	Explain

If three or more of your responses are "No," you may need to rethink whether or not you are ready to complete a traditional benchmarking study.

Worksheet 3.1
Determine Your Readiness for Benchmarking

Instructions: Use the following worksheet to evaluate your organization's readiness to conduct a benchmarking study. Discuss the questions with leaders, colleagues, customers, and stakeholders. Note any significant obstacles. Consider how these obstacles and other factors could affect the benchmarking project.

1. What evidence suggests that we are ready to benchmark?

   • Individuals and teams understand the benchmarking methodologies.

   • Senior leaders and managers have allocated resources to the benchmarking project.

   • Many leaders, managers, and staff indicate a willingness to adapt new practices or processes.

   • The organization has received feedback indicating poor performance.

   • The media or oversight groups tell us we need to improve.

2. Is the initiative related to strategic issues?

   • The process or problem is directly associated with a strategic goal or issue.

   • The organization's efficiency or effectiveness is expected to improve through the benchmarking project.

3. Will our customers or constituents benefit from the results?

   • Customers have given us feedback on the need to improve performance in this area.

   • Customers have given us ideas on how to improve.

   • Customer surveys or measures of complaints indicate a need to improve.

   • Customers have volunteered to help us improve this process or problem.

4. What characterizes the process or problem?

   • Measures collected over time clearly illustrate the problem.

   • Individuals who work on the process express concerns with the process or problem.

Worksheet 3.1 (Continued)

5. Are we prepared to devote the necessary resources to the project?

   - Have staff been advised of the time they will be expected to devote to the project?

   - Have leaders and managers acknowledged in writing that staff time must be allocated to ensure a successful benchmarking project?

   - Have a variety of resources been made available to the benchmarking team, such as travel funds or technical support?

6. What additional questions should my organization consider to determine whether it is ready to benchmark?

   _____

   _____

   _____

Comments about readiness:

_____

_____

_____

_____

_____

Worksheet 3.2
Select the Correct Benchmarking Methodology

Instructions: Check the appropriate box for each statement. Where do your yes answers fall? Note that the availability of resources and the urgency of finding a solution are key factors.

Traditional Benchmarking	Yes	No
1. The problem or process crosses several organizational boundaries.	❏	❏
2. A variety of individuals must be involved for solving the problem or streamlining the process.	❏	❏
3. Extensive data analysis is required.	❏	❏
4. The solution is not supposed to solve an urgent problem or immediate crisis.	❏	❏
5. Performance over time has been inconsistent or poor regardless of prior efforts to improve.	❏	❏
6. A team can be formed and members can dedicate a sufficient amount of time to complete the project.	❏	❏
7. The organization's culture may need to be changed.	❏	❏
8. Various individuals or groups must buy in to the solution.	❏	❏
9. Significant organizational changes are not already under way.	❏	❏

Solution-Driven Benchmarking	Yes	No
1. Time is of the essence.	❏	❏
2. Resources are limited.	❏	❏
3. Implementation of a promising practice is not likely to require a change in the organization's culture.	❏	❏
4. The problem does not cross a large number of organizational boundaries.	❏	❏
5. The leader, manager, or supervisor does not need a lot of buy-in from others to implement the best practice.	❏	❏

Worksheet 4.1
Checklist for the Traditional Benchmarking Method

Instructions: Use this checklist to ensure that all key steps have been completed.

1. Charter a team.

   - ☐ Arrange for the team to receive training on benchmarking.
   - ☐ Draft a team charter if one has not been already created.
   - ☐ Identify a champion or sponsor to help break red tape and bridge organizational boundaries.
   - ☐ Select team members from process owners, managers, and other stakeholder or customer groups.

2. Determine the purpose and scope of the benchmarking initiative.

   - ☐ Review evidence of poor performance.
   - ☐ Identify overall project goals.
   - ☐ Identify stakeholders and long-term outcome.
   - ☐ Write clear statements of purpose and scope, and seek approval or concurrence by stakeholders.

3. Clearly define the process or function you intend to benchmark.

   - ☐ Identify the beginning and end points of the process.
   - ☐ Identify the process owners.
   - ☐ Identify measures of the process.
   - ☐ Add team members when necessary.

4. Research potential benchmarking partners.

   - ☐ Search the Internet for best practices and potential partners.
   - ☐ Contact potential partners to solicit partners, identify measures, and determine the possibility of site visits.

5. Choose performance measures.

   - ☐ Establish criteria for measures.
   - ☐ List measures currently in use and used by partner.

Worksheet 4.1 (Continued)

- ☐ Apply criteria.
- ☐ Select measures.
- ☐ Review IPOLO model to ensure measures fully represent various components.

6. Collect internal data to establish baseline performance.

- ☐ Establish time period for collection processes.
- ☐ Write simple procedures to ensure data are collected consistently over time.
- ☐ Compile data for later analysis.

7. Collect data from partner organization.

- ☐ Ensure time period matches internal data collection time frame.
- ☐ Organize site visit to investigate process differences.
- ☐ Fully research partner organization to prepare for visit.
- ☐ Prepare questions in advance.
- ☐ Be punctual and courteous.
- ☐ Write thank-you notes.

8. Analyze the performance gap between processes.

- ☐ Use graphs and charts to illustrate the differences.
- ☐ Prepare presentations to inform stakeholders and process owners about the benchmarking project, results, and recommendations.
- ☐ Brainstorm reasons for high and low performance.
- ☐ Obtain support for implementation strategies and timelines.

Worksheet 4.1 (Continued)

9. Import practices in order to close the performance gap.

☐ Establish criteria for evaluating and prioritizing practices.

☐ Brainstorm opportunities to strengthen implementation.

☐ Brainstorm obstacles to implementation.

☐ Create an action plan to implement best practices.

10. Regularly monitor results after implementing changes.

☐ Establish clear, regular reporting procedures.

☐ Compile data in a way that displays changes in performance.

☐ Investigate anomalies.

☐ Report to decision makers.

11. Reevaluate changes and start anew.

☐ Identify what worked well about the benchmarking project and what could be improved.

Worksheet 5.1
Solution-Driven Work Steps

Instructions: Complete the following steps to implement a solution-driven benchmarking study.

1. Discover the problem.

   I know this is a problem because _____

   _____

   _____

   List measures that demonstrate the problem.

   a. _____

   b. _____

   c. _____

   d. _____

   e. _____

   Describe the customers or constituents on which this problem has the greatest impact.

   _____

   _____

   What financial costs are associated with this problem?

   _____

   _____

2. Establish criteria for solutions.

   Describe in measurable terms the expectations for performance after the problem is resolved or the process is improved.

   _____

   _____

   Clearly describe the organization or circumstances after the problem is resolved. Be sure to consider the customer's perspective.

   _____

   _____

Worksheet 5.1 (Continued)

3. Search for promising practices. (Refer to Worksheet 5.2: Sources of Promising Practices, for a relational approach to this step.)

List five professional associates or friends who might provide some information or leads on how to resolve this problem or improve the process.

    a. _____

    b. _____

    c. _____

    d. _____

    e. _____

List five professional associations or organizations that might have some information on best practices related to this problem or process.

    a. _____

    b. _____

    c. _____

    d. _____

    e. _____

List additional resources—such as Web pages, renowned experts, publications, or media—that could provide leads on best practices.

    a. _____

    b. _____

    c. _____

    d. _____

    e. _____

Worksheet 5.1 (Continued)

4. Implement promising practices.

   List the individuals who must be involved in importing the best practice.

   a. _____

   b. _____

   c. _____

   d. _____

   e. _____

   Describe obstacles that must be overcome.

   _____

   _____

   _____

   Describe minimum and optimum resources required for implementation.

   _____

   _____

   _____

5. Monitor results.

   List the periods or dates for follow-up _____

   List the person(s) responsible for follow-up.

   a. _____

   b. _____

   c. _____

Worksheet 5.2

Sources for Promising Practices

Instructions: Write a brief problem description in the center circle. Brainstorm and list potential sources of promising or best practices under each heading. Add or customize headings for better application to your organization.

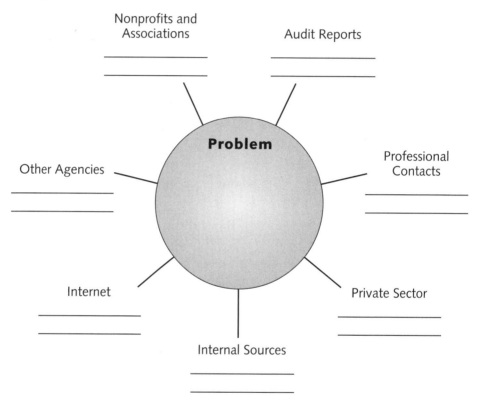

Worksheet 8.1
Are You Ready for International Benchmarking?

Instructions: Consider the following criteria and questions.

1. You are ready (or your organization is ready) for benchmarking an international organization if

   - You have already completed a benchmarking study.
   - You are familiar with both benchmarking methods.
   - You have already researched best practices in the international community.
   - Your organization has international customers or constituents.
   - The global economy affects your organization or constituents.

2. Questions to consider when benchmarking internationally:

   - Do I have the necessary time and resources to conduct a traditional benchmarking study?
   - Will solution-driven benchmarking yield the promising practices that I need to improve?
   - Should I locate partners in my country who can help with an international benchmarking project?
   - What international professional organizations could provide guidance or assistance in my research?
   - Should the geographical location, size of the economy or population, or other demographics influence my choice of a benchmarking partner? My choice of a best practice?

Worksheet 9.1
Evaluate Your Organization's Accountability

Instructions: Rate your organization on each of the following statements to assess the degree of accountability in your organization.

Fiscal Transparency

1. We make our financial records accessible and easy to read for the general public.

1	2	3	4	5
Never		Sometimes		Usually

2. The results of benchmarking and other tools have been published and reported regardless of the unattractive nature of the results.

1	2	3	4	5
Never		Sometimes		Usually

Increased Internal Accountability

3. Benchmarking and other tools have been used to identify low performing areas and find best practices to show demonstrable improvements.

1	2	3	4	5
Never		Sometimes		Usually

4. Management clearly communicates to staff members their job responsibilities and expectations.

1	2	3	4	5
Never		Sometimes		Usually

Improved Public Relations

5. Opportunities are provided for clients or citizens to express their opinions and preferences.

1	2	3	4	5
Never		Sometimes		Usually

Worksheet 9.1 (Continued)

6. Customer surveys and other feedback mechanisms are used to improve and demonstrate measurable improvement over time.

1	2	3	4	5
Never		Sometimes		Usually

Better Preparation for a Crisis

7. We have identified potential natural disaster crises that could occur in our area (flood, earthquake, wildfire, hurricane) and have identified potential benchmark partners who have experienced a similar crisis.

1	2	3	4	5
Never		Sometimes		Usually

8. Our organization is continually scanning its peers, professional organizations, and the media for issues or events that could adversely affect it.

1	2	3	4	5
Never		Sometimes		Usually

Enhanced Decision Making

9. We use benchmarking to identify a wide range of solutions and to solve problems.

1	2	3	4	5
Never		Sometimes		Usually

10. Leaders and managers are provided with the results of benchmarking or other analytical tools when they are faced with major organizational decisions.

1	2	3	4	5
Never		Sometimes		Usually

Creation of a Learning Organization

11. Our organization adapts and revises our benchmarking methodology in an effort to become more effective.

1	2	3	4	5
Never		Sometimes		Usually

12. Our organization has adapted to the changing environment as evidenced by new policies and procedures that reduce costs or improve customer products and services.

1	2	3	4	5
Never		Sometimes		Usually

Accountability Score

54–60	Highly accountable organization
48–53	Good level of accountability
42–47	Fair level of accountability
36–41	Poor level of accountability
35 and below	Definitely needs improvement

Worksheet 10.1
Integrate Solution-Driven Benchmarking
into the Audit Plan

Instructions: Use this worksheet to formulate the questions *related to solution-driven benchmarking* that must be answered in each of the major audit steps.

Plan

1. _____

   _____

2. _____

   _____

3. _____

   _____

Objectives

1. _____

   _____

2. _____

   _____

3. _____

   _____

Scope

1. _____

   _____

2. _____

   _____

3. _____

   _____

Worksheet 10.1 (Continued)

Staff

1. _____

_____

2. _____

_____

3. _____

_____

Data collection and analysis

1. _____

_____

2. _____

_____

3. _____

_____

Recommendations

1. _____

_____

2. _____

_____

3. _____

_____

Worksheet 10.2
Write Audit Steps for Solution-Driven Benchmarking

Instructions: Describe in the audit stages below any unique steps or issues that must be addressed for a successful solution-driven benchmarking study.

1. Plan _____

   _____

   _____

2. Objectives _____

   _____

3. Scope _____

4. Staff _____

   _____

   _____

5. Data collection and analysis _____

   _____

   _____

6. Results analysis _____

   _____

   _____

7. Recommendations _____

   _____

   _____

8. Report preparation and distribution _____

   _____

Worksheet 10.3
Elements of a Finding Linked to Solution-Driven Benchmarking

Instructions: Review the Elements of a Finding and the Link to Solution-Driven Benchmarking. Then note in the spaces below the evidence that you will collect or have already collected to document the finding.

Elements of a Finding	Link to Solution-Driven Benchmarking
Condition	Convincing evidence or information that leads to the auditee's willingness to search for best or promising practices.
Criteria	Measures already used by the benchmarking partner that strongly indicate performance could be improved if a best practice were imported to the auditee's organization.
Cause	Lack of a best or promising practice in the auditee that results in poor performance.
Effect	Difference between current low performance by the auditee and the potentially high performance already accomplished by the partner if the auditee imports a best practice.
Recommendations	Actions taken to import the best or promising practice.

Recommendations

1. Condition: _____

   _____

2. Criteria: _____

   _____

3. Cause: _____

   _____

4. Effect: _____

   _____

5. Recommendations: _____

   _____

GLOSSARY

Accountability	The principle that individuals and organizations are responsible for their actions and decisions. When actions and decisions appear questionable, people have the right to ask that those behaviors be explained to others.
Benchmark	A point of reference to which other information is compared; standard.
Benchmarking	A methodology used by individuals and teams to define a problem or process, locate organizations that have already addressed the problem or improved the process, determine how the organization improved, and import the practice to the home organization.
Benchmarking champion	A senior leader who becomes the strongest advocate for the benchmarking project and thus plays a pivotal role in its success.
Customer satisfaction	A measure of how products and services supplied by a government or nonprofit organization meet or surpass customer expectations. It is seen as a key performance indicator in the public sector.
Effectiveness	Ability to achieve stated goals; long-term impact of outputs, processes, and expenditures or inputs.
Efficiency	The ratio of outputs to inputs (resources allocated); productivity. Efficiency is a fairly narrow term that does not include measures of cycle time or quality.
Error rate	The number of errors in a product or service compared to the total possible errors or the total number of products or services delivered.

Government Performance and Results Act of 1993	Legislation intended to (a) improve federal program effectiveness and public accountability, (b) improve internal management of the federal government, and (c) improve the confidence of the American people in the capability of the federal government. It also mandates that each agency head submit to the director of the Office of Management and Budget and to the Congress a strategic plan for program activities and measures to demonstrate performance improvement.
Inputs	Resources expended to complete work; dollars; cost of materials and computers. For data analysis the number of full-time-equivalent (FTE) staff may be used as a substitute for staff salaries.
Learning organization	An organization that uses benchmarking methods regularly to evaluate its processes and performance measures and to incorporate best practices into its own. This practice helps employees to develop skills that allow them to adapt to a changing environment.
Link	A logical, intuitive or empirical connection, presumably causal although not proven, between producing outputs and the ultimate outcome.
Mandatory Performance Measurement Program (MPMP)	An initiative launched in 2000 by the government of Ontario, Canada, that requires municipalities to report annually on fifty-four measures of effectiveness and efficiency in twelve key service areas. It is designed to strengthen local accountability by keeping citizens informed about municipal service plans, standards, costs, and value.
Nonprofit	An organization whose primary objective is to support an issue or matter of private interest or public concern for noncommercial purposes, without concern for monetary profit. The nonprofit sector is also referred to as the third sector, voluntary sector, independent sector, or charitable sector, and nonprofit organizations may also be referred to as nongovernmental organizations (NGOs).
Outcome	The long-term impact of outputs, process, and expenditures. *Outcome* is frequently used interchangeably with *effectiveness*. For example, anticipated outcomes of DARE programs may include increased knowledge about drugs and alcohol, changed attitudes about drugs and alcohol, and reduced involvement with drugs and alcohol.

Outcome evaluation	An evaluation that identifies the net effects of a program after a specified period of operation. It seeks to answer the management question, "What difference did the program make?" It tells management about (a) the extent to which the problems and needs that gave rise to the program still exist, (b) ways to ameliorate adverse impacts and enhance desirable impacts, and (c) program design adjustments that may be indicated for the future.
Output	Units of work produced; at the end of the day, week, or month, the volume of products or services provided; the immediate result of a process. For example, the output of a drug enforcement team may include the amount of marijuana shipments seized, the number of drug rings investigated, and the number of drug arrests made.
Partner	An organization that serves as the point of comparison for the organization that is conducting a benchmarking study.
Performance evaluation	An assessment of individuals or organizations to determine whether changes are necessary to improve performance.
Performance management	Day-to-day decision making with the goal of improving the individual's or organization's ability to produce products and services or operate efficiently and accomplish goals. Organizations use performance measures and standards strategically to establish performance targets, to prioritize and allocate resources, to inform managers about needed adjustments in policy or program directions to meet goals, to frame reports on success in meeting performance goals, and to improve quality.
Performance measurement	Regular and consistent collection of data to determine if a program is operating efficiently and effectively and is producing products and services that are timely and meet the customer's expectations. Performance measure categories include inputs, outputs, operational measures, error rates, cycle times, customer satisfaction scores, complaints, and outcomes. In general, pre- and post-comparisons are used to assess change.
Performance measures	Numbers that represent the degree to which a program has achieved stated objectives and goals. They include inputs, outputs, operational measures, error rates, cycle times, customer satisfaction scores, complaints, and outcomes.

Process	A series of steps or activities on which resources are expended, resulting in the delivery of a product or service. A variety of performance measures represent process efficiency, timeliness, and error rate.
Process evaluation	An analysis of the work steps, policies, and procedures necessary to produce a product or service. It tends to focus on outputs rather than the appropriateness or accomplishment of long-term goals.
Process owners	The people most familiar with the process, those who can provide valuable answers to certain questions as they arise in the benchmarking process.
Quality	A characteristic of a product or service that is measured in terms of number of errors or relative customer satisfaction.
Sarbanes-Oxley Act	Federal legislation passed in 2002 to improve accountability and transparency in the private sector (in response to Enron and other corporate scandals). It has also influenced the nonprofit and public sectors, encouraging better auditing procedures.
Solution-driven benchmarking	A five-step, streamlined method of benchmarking in which the problem is quickly identified and analyzed. It is highly dependent on a network of professional contacts or associations who can quickly identify best or promising practices.
Stakeholders	Someone who directly or indirectly holds an interest in something.
Total quality management	A customer-focused management philosophy and strategy that seeks continuous improvement in business processes by using analytical tools and teamwork that encompasses all employees.
Traditional benchmarking	An eleven-step method of benchmarking that requires an in-depth analysis of current processes, practices, and performance measures, and a comparison to another organization to locate ways to improve.
Transparency	The full, accurate, and timely disclosure of information. Usually used in reference to fiscal transparency, making it easier for citizens to review revenue and expenditures. Transparency is a key element in increasing an organization's public accountability.
Web 2.0	Collectively, the numerous Web-based communities and online social networks that are making the World Wide Web more interactive.

REFERENCES

America's Second Harvest. (2007). [Mission statement.] Retrieved October 25, 2007, from www.secondharvest.org/about_us/our_mission.html.

American Water Works Association Research Foundation. (2007). [Web site.] Retrieved October 19, 2007, from www.awwarf.org.

Ammons, D. (2001). *Municipal benchmarks: Assessing local performance and establishing community standards* (2nd ed.). Thousand Oaks, CA: Sage.

Anheier, H. K. (2005). *Nonprofit organizations: Theory, management, policy.* London: Routledge.

Asian Development Bank. (2006). *Pro-poor services delivery initiatives by Bangalore Mahanagara Palike.* Retrieved on November 12, 2007, from www.adb.org/Governance/Pro_poor/Urban_case/PDF/Bang_Exec_Sum.pdf.

Association of Local Government Auditors (ALGA). (2002). *Report on NALGA's benchmarking and best practices survey for fiscal year 2002.* Lexington, KY: Author.

Association of Pacific Islands Public Auditors. (2003). History. Retrieved November 15, 2007, from http://apipa.guamopa.org.

Baldrige National Quality Program, National Institute of Standards and Technology. (2007). *Criteria for performance excellence.* Retrieved October 27, 2007, from www.quality.nist.gov/Business_Criteria.htm.

Bertelsmann-Stiftung. (2004). Encouraging social change. Carl Bertelsmann Prize: Improving performance and progress in the public sector—Organizational culture and leadership. Retrieved January 23, 2008, from http://www.bertelsmann-stiftung.de/cps/rde/xchg/SID-0A000F14-DB5D4D43/bst_engl/hs.xsl/prj_6983_7005.htm.

Burke, J. (2005, June). Ontario's Municipal Performance Measurement Program: Fostering innovation and accountability in local government. *Government Finance Review.*

Camp, R. C. (1998). *Global cases in benchmarking.* Milwaukee: ASQ Quality Press.

Carmona, R. (2003). *The obesity crisis in America.* Testimony before the Subcommittee on Education, Reform Committee on Education, and the Workforce Committee. U.S.

House of Representatives. Retrieved November 12, 2007, from www.surgeongeneral
.gov/news/testimony/obesity07162003.htm.

City of Austin. (2007). Austin city connection: ePerformance measures. Retrieved October 25, 2007, from www.ci.austin.tx.us/budget/eperf/index.cfm.

Community of Metros. (2007). Community of Metros: CoMET. Retrieved November 12, 2007, from www.comet-metros.org.

Cumberland County Pennsylvania. (2007, April 19). *Cumberland County receives award for budget reforms* [Press release]. Retrieved October 19, 2007, from www.ccpa.net/cumber land/lib/cumberland/commissioners_newscenter/Strategy_and_Budget_Award.pdf.

DavisWiki. (2007). [Home page]. Retrieved October 27, 2007, from http://daviswiki.org.

Discovery Gateway. (2006, September 15). [Press release]. Retrieved October 25, 2007, from www.childmuseum.org/resources/docs/press_091506.doc.

Discovery Gateway. (2007). [Mission statement]. Retrieved October 25, 2007, from www .childmuseum.org/aboutus/press.html.

Doades, R. (1992). Making the best of best practices. *Public Utilities Fortnightly, 130*(4), 15–18.

Festen, M., & Philbin, M. (2007). *Level best: How small and grassroots nonprofits can tackle evaluation and talk results.* San Francisco: Jossey-Bass.

Frumkin, P., & Imber, J. B. (Eds.). (2004). *In search of the nonprofit sector.* New Brunswick, CT: Transaction.

Ghobadian, A., & Speller, S. (1994). Gurus of quality: A framework for comparison. *Total Quality Management, 5*(3), 53–70.

Gore, A. (1993). *Creating a government that works better and costs less: The report of the National Performance Review.* New York: Plume.

GuideStar. (2007). About us. Retrieved October 27, 2007, from www.guidestar.org/about/ index.jsp?source=dnabout.

Henderson, S. (2007). City manager promotes economic development in Bulgaria. City of Golden [Web site]. Retrieved November 14, 2007, from http://ci.golden.co.us/News .asp?NewsID=211.

Howard, M., & Killmartin, B. (2006). *Assessment of benchmarking within government orga-nizations.* Retrieved October 24, 2007, from www.nasact.org/downloads/Assessment% 20of%20Benchmarking%20Within%20Govt%20Orgs%20July%202006.pdf.

Independent Sector. (2006). The Sarbanes-Oxley Act and implications for nonprofit orga-nizations. Retrieved November 15, 2007, from www.independentsector.org/PDFs/ sarbanesoxley.pdf.

Independent Sector. (2007). Who we are and what we do. Retrieved November 15, 2007, from www.independentsector.org/about/index.html.

Internal Revenue Service. (March 2007). Internal Revenue Service Data Book 2006. Publi-cation 55B, p. 56. Washington, D.C. http://www.irs.gov/pub/irs-soi/06databk.pdf.

International City/County Management Association. (2004). *Performance management: When results matter.* Washington, DC: Author.

International City/County Management Association. (2007a). *Center for Performance Measurement & its mission.* Retrieved October 13, 2007, from www.icma.org/main/bc.asp?bcid=108&hsid=1&ssid1=50&ssid2=220&ssid3=302.

International City/County Management Association. (2007b). *Comparative performance measurement program.* Retrieved October 13, 2007, from www.icma.org/main/bc.asp?bcid=107&hsid=1&ssid1=50&ssid2=220&ssid3=297.

Kettl, D. F. (1998). *Reinventing government: A fifth-year report card.* Washington, DC: Brookings Institution.

Kraft, J. (1997). *The Department of the Navy benchmarking handbook* (TQLO Publication No. 97–03). Washington, DC: Department of the Navy, Total Quality Leadership Office.

Kwok, A. (1993, Sept. 9). Phoenix sitting on top of world as best-run city. [Final Chaser edition]. *The Arizona Republic,* p.A1.

M+R Strategic Services & Advocacy Institute. (2006). *The e-nonprofit benchmarks study.* Retrieved October 25, 2007, from www.e-benchmarksstudy.com.

Moe, R. C. (1994). The "reinventing government" exercise: Misinterpreting the problem, misjudging the consequences. *Public Administration Review, 54*(2), 111–122.

National Partnership for Reinventing Government. (2001, Jan. 19). [Archived home page]. Retrieved October 8, 2007, from http://govinfo.library.unt.edu/npr/index.htm.

Neighbor, H. (2001). *Niger benchmarking study: Harmonizing decentralized financial management.* Washington, D.C.: Africa Rural Development.

New study looks at property taxes and financing local government in Lake County. (2005, March 3). *Indiana University News Room.* Retrieved November 12, 2007, from http://newsinfo.iu.edu/news/page/normal/1960.html. For more information on Lake County, Indiana, see http://www.ibrc.indiana.edu/lakegov/interface.htm.

Office of the Federal Environmental Executive. (2007). *Green purchasing: Environmentally benign adhesives.* Retrieved October 27, 2007, from www.ofee.gov/gp/eba.asp.

Office of Legislative Auditor General & Welsh, W. L. (2000–2001). *Best practices for good management.* Retrieved October 9, 2007, from http://le.state.ut.us/audit/00_2001rpt.pdf.

O'Neill, M. (2002). *Nonprofit nation: A new look at the third America.* San Francisco: Jossey-Bass.

Ontario Centre for Municipal Best Practices. (2004, February). *Best practice report: Urban transit: Alternative service delivery: Trans-cab* [Case study for the City of Hamilton: Hamilton Street Railway]. Toronto: Author.

Ontario Centre for Municipal Best Practices. (2007). *Mandate.* Retrieved October 24, 2007, from www.amo.on.ca/AM/Template.cfm?Section=About_Us4.

Oregon Progress Board. (1991, Jan.). Oregon benchmarks: Setting measurable standards for progress. (Report to the 1991 Oregon Legislature.) Salem, OR: Author.

Osborne, D. E., & Gaebler, T. (1992). *Reinventing government: How the entrepreneurial spirit is transforming the public sector.* Reading, MA: Addison-Wesley.

Ott, J. S. (Ed.). (2001). *The nature of the nonprofit sector.* Boulder, CO: Westview Press.

Park City Municipal Corporation. (2007). "Citizens budget: A guide to the fiscal year 2008 municipal budget," p.2.

Patrick, R., & Kozlosky, C. (2006). *Benchmarking water utilities customer relations best practices.* Denver, CO: American Water Works Association Research Foundation.

Pegnato, J. A. (1997). Is a citizen a customer? *Public Productivity & Management Review, 20*(4), 397–404.

Pennsylvania Department of Community and Economic Development. (2007). *Governor's award for local government excellence.* Retrieved October 24, 2007, from www .newpa.com/default.aspx?id=142.

Poister, T. H. (2003). *Measuring performance in public and nonprofit organizations.* San Francisco: Jossey-Bass.

Poister, T. H., & Streib, G. (1994). Municipal management tools from 1976 to 1993: An overview and update. *Public Productivity & Management Review, 18*(2), 115–125.

Poister, T. H., & Streib, G. (1999). Performance measurement in municipal government: Assessing the state of practice. *Public Administration Review, 59*(4), 325–335.

Pollak, T. H., & Blackwood, A. (2007). "Facts and figures from the Nonprofit Almanac 2007." Washington, D.C.: Urban Institute. www.urban.org/url.cfm?ID-311373.

Resort Community Benchmarking Group. (2006). Resort community benchmarking report. Park City, UT: Author.

Salt Lake County, Utah. (2007). County option funding for zoological, cultural, and botanical organizations, known as the Zoo, Arts, & Parks Program. (Salt Lake County Wide Policy no. 1031.) Retrieved November 15, 2007, from www.slcozap.org/zapArts/pdf/ZAPPolicy1031207.pdf.

Segal, G., & Summers, A. (2002). Citizens' budget reports: Improving performance and accountability in government. Policy study no. 292. Los Angeles: Reason Public Policy Institute.

Shaping America's Youth. (2006). Shaping America's Youth challenges Americans working to reduce childhood obesity to participate in online registry. Retrieved November 15, 2007, from www.shapingamericasyouth.org/pressrelease.pdf?pressreleaseid=54.

Shister, G. (2007, May 13). Young adults eschew traditional nightly news for "The Daily Show." *Philadelphia Inquirer.*

Smith, S. R., & Lipsky, M. (1993). *Nonprofits for hire: The welfare state in the age of contracting.* Cambridge, MA: Harvard University Press.

Southern Utah Recycling Coalition. (2007).[Home page.] Retrieved November 15, 2007, from http://southernutahrecyles.org.

Thompson, J. R. (2000). Reinvention as reform: Assessing the National Performance Review. *Public Administration Review, 60*(6), 508–521.

UNC [University of North Carolina] School of Government, North Carolina Benchmarking Project. (2007). [Web site.] Retrieved October 24, 2007, from www.iog.unc.edu/programs/perfmeas.

Urban Institute, National Center for Charitable Statistics. (2007). *Number of nonprofit organizations in the United States, 1996–2006.* Retrieved October 25, 2007, from http://nccsdataweb.urban.org/PubApps/profile1.php?state=US.

U.S. Department of the Interior, Office of Inspector General. (2004). *Fleet management operations: U.S. Department of the Interior* (C-IN-MOA-0042–2003). Washington, DC: Author.

U.S. Department of Justice, Office of the Inspector General. (2004). A review of the FBI's handling of intelligence information related to the September 11 attacks. Retrieved November 14, 2007, from www.usdoj.gov/oig/special/s0606/final.pdf.

U.S. Environmental Protection Agency. (2006). *Site-specific charging at Superfund: Benchmarking regional practices.* Washington, DC: Author.

U.S. Government Accountability Office. (1995). General services administration: Opportunities for cost savings and service improvements (T-GGD-95–96). Retrieved November 12, 2007, from archive.gao.gov/t2pbat1/153881.pdf.

U.S. Government Accountability Office. (2003). *Government auditing standards: 2003 revision* (GAO-03–673G). Retrieved October 28, 2007, from www.gao.gov/govaud/yb2003.pdf.

U.S. Government Accountability Office. (2005). *IRS needs better strategic planning and evaluation of taxpayer assistance training* (GAO-05–782). Retrieved October 28, 2007, from www.gao.gov/cgi-bin/getrpt?GAO-05-782.

U.S. Government Accountability Office. (2007). *Federal Retirement Thrift Investment Board: Due diligence over administrative expenses should continue and be broadened* (GAO-07–541). Retrieved October 28, 2007, from www.gao.gov/cgi-bin/getrpt?GAO-07-541.

U.S. Postal Service Office of the Inspector General. (2007). Audit report. Retrieved November 14, 2007, from www.uspsoig.gov/FOIA_files/HM-AR-07-002.pdf.

Utah Benchmarking Project. (2007, April). Report presented at the Utah City Management Association meeting, St. George, UT.

Utah Food Bank. (2006). *Annual Report 2006.* Salt Lake City, UT. Retrieved November 15, 2007, from www.utahfoodbank.org/images/stories/pdf/06annualreport.pdf.

Utah State Office of Education. (2007). Child and Adult Care Food Program. Retrieved November 15, 2007, from www.usoe.k12.ut.us/cnp/CACFP/default.asp.

VisitScotland.com. (2007). Benchmarking reports. Retrieved November 12, 2007, from www.visitscotland.org/research_and_statistics/other_research_reports/benchmarking_scotland/benchmark.htm.

Walden, R. M. (2005, Sept. 25). The Red Cross money pit [Editorial]. *Los Angeles Times.*

Whitney, S. (2006, September 15). A new discovery. *Deseret Morning News.* Retrieved October 25, 2007, from http://findarticles.com/p/articles/mi_qn4188/is_20060915/ai_n16738947.

Williams, S. E. (1998). National Australian local government benchmarking project. In R. C. Camp, (Ed.), *Global cases in benchmarking: Best practices from organizations around the world.* Milwaukee: ASQ Quality Press.

INDEX

A

Accountability: benchmarking for improving, 161–170; benefits of benchmarking for, 164–170; examples of increased attention to, 162–164; federal legislation for improving, 163; fiscal transparency in, 165–166; internal, increased through benchmarking, 166–167; internal and taxpayer in public sector, 110; in nonprofit sector, 163–164; principle of, 162; of public and nonprofit executives, 162; and public trust, 161; of state and local governments, 110–111; worksheet for evaluating, 216–218

Administrative staff, as key benchmarking team players, 120–121

America's Second Harvest, 139; determining performance measurement indicators in, 144; mission of, 143; networking and network activity report of, 144; selection of benchmarking partners in, 144

American Water Works Association Research Foundation (AwwaRF), benchmarking for customer satisfaction in, 108–109, 111

Ammons, D., 110

Anheier, H. K., 127

Association of Local Government Auditors (ALGA), benchmarking and best practices surveys, 177

Association of Pacific Islands Public Auditors, and incorporation of best practices in program audits, 149

Audit plan: and audit objectives, 184; determination of audit scope in, 184; staffing concerns in, 184–185; standards and guidelines for steps in, 183; use of solution-driven method in, 183–186

Audit staff, as key benchmarking team players, 120–121

Auditor recommendations, 178; as actions to be taken, 176; development of 185; organizations' obligation to consider, 174

Audits: assurance of well-grounded findings in, 174; basic benchmarking skills for conducting, 175–176; benchmarking of auditor's own process in, 177; data collection and analysis in, 176, 185; development of comparative conditions in, 177–178; and development of a finding, 175; establishing criteria for solutions in, 181;

integration of solution-driven method in, 182–183; research in, 175; searching for and implementing promising practices in, 181–182; solution-driven benchmarking method used in, 179–182; and tasks required for benchmarking, 173–174; using traditional benchmarking in, 176–179

Austin, Texas, public links to city management strategies in, 118–119

Australia's Local Government Ministers' Conference, multifaceted benchmarking studies and best practices in, 152–153

Award programs, as reliable sources of promising practice, 23–24

B

Baldrige National Quality Program, overview of, 14

Bangalore, India, successful benchmarking initiatives in, 156

Barcellos, S., 20

Benchmark, defining, 11–12

Benchmark training costs, 21

Benchmarking: auditors' unique role in, 174; areas for future research in, 189–190; common steps in, 13; and continuous improvement, 19, 74; data collection challenges in, 82; evaluation focus in, 42–43; enhanced decision-making process for, 169–170; formal training in, 191; historical context of, 12–16; idea of importing practices in, 18, 21–22; implementation, and stakeholders' buy-in, 190; importance of sustaining momentum of, 188–189; and internal accountability, 166–167; Internet's impact on, 18–19; as key management tool in state/local

governments, 123; necessity of monitoring and measuring, 187–188; and organization's unique characteristics, 191; performance indicators in, 14; and public/nonprofit entities' accountability, 164; recalibration as standard operating practice in, 74; and resistance to change, 72; roles of department and division heads in, 119–120; scope creep in, 67; search for best practices in, 14; technological advances and need to reevaluate, 141; and transition to learning organization, 170

Benchmarking challenges, 79–82; and adoption of streamlined method, 83; hurdles and delays as, 81–82; in implementation, 82; *industrial tourist* syndrome as, 80; self-deception trap in, 80–81

Benchmarking champions, expectations of, 120

Benchmarking learning process, stages in, 188–189

Benchmarking measures: process and output categories in, 42–43; role in traditional versus solution-driven method in, 58; selection of, 42–43, 204

Benchmarking methods/methodologies: compared by characteristics, 56–59; conceptual differences between types of, 54–56; and continuous improvement, 190; lack of documented success in, 190; and organization size, 58–59; resource requirements in, 58; selection of, 53–60; in training programs, 17; and transition from TQM to reinvention, 15–16; worksheet for selecting, 207

Benchmarking models, 64

Benchmarking partners: choosing similar and appropriate stakeholders as, 114–115; identifying and selecting, 68; roles of, 13

Benchmarking preparations, 49–61; consideration of desired outcomes and strategic goals in, 51; and customer/constituent benefits, 51–52; focus on critical and strategic processes in, 60–61; method selection in, 53–60; pitfalls to avoid, 60–61; readiness assessment steps in, 49–53; and resource needs, 52–53; selection of processes in, 60; weighing costs and benefits in, 52; worksheet for determining readiness in, 205–206

Benchmarking taxonomy, need for developing, 189–190

Benchmarking teams: implementation plan of, 13; important activities of, 65–66; member selection process in, 65; tasks of, 53–54

Best practices, 15; award programs as, 23–24; defining/use of term, 13, 21, 22; early promotion of, 21–22; emerging industry trends and, 23; evolving attitudes toward, 21–22; importing successfully, 73–74; local government's early focus on, 104; and performance-based budgeting, 23; search for, 88; self-declared, 22; sources of, 22–24

Blackwood, A., 128, 129

Bradley, J., 136

Budget staff, as key team players, 120–121

Bullock, K., 110

Burke, J., 107

C

Camp, R. C., 12, 153

Carl Bertelsmann Prize, performance-based competition for, 24

Carmona, R., 169

Christensen, M., 117

Citizen surveys, as measure of quality, 38

Citizens, public sector benchmarking access for, 118–119

CoMET (Community of Metros) benchmarking studies, 154–155; establishment of common measures and best practices in, 155

Conover, J., 168

Continuous improvement practice, 97; and solution-driven benchmarking method, 19

Corporate benchmarking method, 64

Crisis preparations, benchmarking and best practices in, 168–169

Cumberland County, Pennsylvania, Fiscal Accountability and Best Management Practices award for, 110–111

Customer satisfaction, as key purpose for benchmarking projects, 108–110

Customers, public sector benchmarking roles of, 118–119

D

Definitions and basic concepts, worksheet for, 198–199

Department of the Navy Benchmarking Handbook (Kraft), 64

Desired outcomes: identifying, 29; linked to outputs, 29–30

Developing countries, U.S. financial support for benchmarking in, 20

Discovery Gateway (Utah Children's Museum): best and promising practices in design process, 138; research and evaluation process in design of, 137–138; solution-driven benchmarking steps of, 138–139

E

Efficiency, as fundamental goal for benchmarking, 107–108

Eichelberger, G., 111

Elected officials: and benchmarking for accountability, 162–164; and benchmarking readiness assessment, 118; public sector benchmarking roles of, 118

Eleven-step traditional benchmarking method, 64–74; data requests in, 70–71; defining process/function to be benchmarked in, 67–68; defining purpose and scope of, 66–67; examples of, 74–79; importance of completing all steps in, 69; importing and adapting best practices in, 71–72; need for continuous improvement in, 81; new best practice implementation in, 72–73; reconsideration of measurement system in, 73; summary of, 65*fig*4.1

eNonprofit Benchmarks Study: sources of data and statistics for, 141–142; use of e-mail for advocacy in, 142

F

Federal government, TQM and process improvement in, 15

Federal government benchmarking: and private sector's benchmarking influence, 104; and training activities, 19. *See also specific agency*

Federal Quality Institute (FQI), promotion of TQM by, 15

Federal Retirement Thrift Investment Board (FRTIB), GAO criticism of benchmarking methods used by, 178

Festen, M., 133

Fiscal transparency: in public and nonprofit accountability, 165–166; and user-friendly budgets, 165

Foster children placement, benchmarking study on, 94–95

Frumkin, P., 127

G

Gaebler, T., 15, 108

Ghobadian, A., 12

Gomes, D., 143

Government agencies, evolving use of performance measures in, 39–40. *See also specific agency*

Government Auditing Standards, 183

Government executives, global benchmarking activities of, 103

Government Performance and Results Act (GPRA), 16

Graduate School, USDA, Government Audit Training Institute: Executive Leadership Program's snow removal benchmarking study, 93–94; Pacific Islands Training Initiative/Virgin Islands Training Initiative (PITI/VITI) for knowledge- and skill-building of public sector employees, 148–150; Performance Auditing course, 174–175

Guam Memorial Hospital Authority (GMHA), 20; benchmarking readiness in, 49, 50; successful solution-driven benchmarking in, 89–91

Guam's Island Government Finance Officers Association: promotion of benchmarking tool in, 150; solution-driven method use by, 150

GuideStar database, and fiscal transparency, 165

H

Harris, J., 92

Hartman, D., 78

Henderson, S., 20

Howard, M., 103, 106, 111

I

ICMA's Center for Performance Measurement, 24

Medlin, S., 34, 51
Missouri Accountability Portal (MAP), 166
Moe, R. C., 108
Municipal management, use of informal measurement process in, 40–41

N

National associations, organization and facilitation of benchmarking studies by, 106
National Partnership for Reinventing Government, 15
Neighbor, H., 154
Niger, World Bank's commissioned benchmarking study of, 154
No Child Left Behind Act, 33
Nongovernmental organizations, solution-driven benchmarking of, 18–19
Nonprofit sector: categories of, 128–129; corporate donor ties to, 132; creative problem-solving practice in, 136–137; defined, 128–129; estimated size of, 128; financial and administrative resource limits in, 136; government grants as revenue source for, 132; growth of, 1960–2000, 129; historical reliance on instinct in, 133; as incubator for solutions, 136; independent sector in, 128; magnitude and influence of, 129–132; and nondistribution constraint, 128; performance management process in, 44; and public accountability, 132; revenues generated in, 129; unique and diverse organizations in, 129
Nonprofit sector benchmarking: accountability pressures in, 124; adoption of, 12; board members' role in, 134; competition and communication in, 135; congressional actions addressing

accountability in, 163–164; discovery process in, 133; examples of, 135–141; fiscal transparency in, 165; leadership as basis of first step in, 134; model of performance measures and strategic purpose for, 28–31; pressures and responses to benchmark in, 132–133; search for best practices in, 127; solution-driven approach to, 18, 128, 133–134; streamlined approach in, 134
North Carolina Benchmarking Project, broad coalition and process in, 113–114

O

O'Neill, M., 127, 129
Ontario, Canada, municipalities: Mandatory Performance Measurement Program in, 107–108; and provincial government partnership with, 107–108
Oregon state government benchmarking: emphasis on outcomes and partnerships in, 104; incorporating general public in, 118; setting and publishing of performance standards by, 104–105; unique approach of, 105
Organization size, and benchmarking method, 58–59
Organizational cultural change, solution-driven benchmarking resulting from, 97
Organizational learning, simple model for, 188
Osborne, D. E., 15, 108
Outcome measures: defined, 39; links between outputs and, 38, 39; and long-term strategies and goals, 38
Output measures, as benchmarking focus, 42–43
Outputs: and achievement of outcomes, 29, 32–33, 38; defined, 34–35; and

desired outcomes, 29–30; determination of, 29; multiple, need for, 33

P

T

Technology, facilitation of benchmarking through, 17, 18–19

Thompson, J. R., 108

Total quality management (TQM), 12–13, 14

Traditional benchmarking method, 17; auditors' use of, 176–179; benefits of, 63; checklists for, 208–210; compared with solution-driven method, 53–59; complexity of, 57; discovery and defining of problem in, 86–87; examples of, 74–79; and faulty processes as source of organization's problem, 58; five steps in, 87; identifying and evaluating important measures in, 63; and implementation of proven best practices, 63–64; involvement of managers and leaders in, 57–58; simple and sequential actions in, 64; steps in, 53–54, 86–89. *See also* Eleven-step traditional benchmarking method

Transformation of function, benchmarking for, 111

U

U.S. Department of the Interior (DOI): benchmarking study of royalty management programs, 78–79; benchmarking training in, 20; and search for promising practices, 182

U.S. Environmental Protection Agency (EPA): benchmarking project in, 19; Program Assessment Review Tool (PART), 52–53; Superfund benchmarking evaluation, 74–75

U.S. General Services Administration (GSA), benchmarking in, 41

U.S. Government Accountability Office (GAO): criticisms of benchmarking studies, 178; reason for name change of, 162–163; use of performance measures in, 39–40

U.S. Postal Service, benchmarking for internal accountability in, 166–167

USDA Child & Adult Care Food Program (CACFP), 140–141

USDA executive development programs, benchmarking projects in, 19

Utah Benchmarking Project: defined purpose of, 116; leaders' pivotal role in, 120; organizations involved in, 115; participating partners in, 116; survey instrument created in, 116–117; use of technology in, 71

Utah Food Bank Services (UFBS), 139, 140; accountability to donors and volunteers in, 140; formal and informal benchmarking in, 139–140; internal performance measures used in, 140, 141; services and service delivery in, 139, 140

Utah's Zoo, Arts, and Parks Tax, nonprofits' solution-driven approach to, 135–136

W

Walden, R. M., 161

Web 2.0 communication advances, 23. *See also* Internet and Web–based communication

Welsh, W., 22

Whitney, S., 138

Wiki online communities, public sector use of, 23

Williams, S. E., 153

X

Xerox benchmarking methodology, overview of, 13